I0840767

Places

I'm Going To
Go Back There,

Some Day

by
The Lonesome Hillbilly

Books by the same author

The Book on Motorcycle Camping
How to Live on the Road Full Time

Places: I'm Going to Go Back There, Some Day

Roads: All Roads Lead to Roam

Friends: Two-Legs, Four-Legs, Six-Legs, Wings and Roots

Visions: Things and Ideas Found in the Wild

Elements: Elemental, Elementary

Things in Heaven and Earth
Essays from Places, Roads, Friends, Visions and Elements
with full-color illustrations

Dedicated to
Sacagawea "Bird Woman"
Because everyone needs a guide

Contents

The Sea And the Hills
by Rudyard Kipling

Who hath desired the Sea? –
  the sight of salt water unbounded–
The heave and the halt and the hurl
  and the crash of the comber wind-hounded?
The sleek-barrelled swell before storm,
  grey, foamless, enormous, and growing
Stark calm on the lap of the Line
  or the crazy-eyed hurricane blowing –
His Sea in no showing the same -
  his Sea and the same 'neath each showing:
  His Sea as she slackens or thrills?
So and no otherwise – so and no otherwise –
  hillmen desire their Hills!

Who hath desired the Sea? –
  the immense and contemptuous surges?
The shudder, the stumble, the swerve,
  as the star-stabbing bow-sprit emerges?
The orderly clouds of the Trades,
  the ridged, roaring sapphire thereunder –
Unheralded cliff-haunting flaws
  and the headsail's low-volleying thunder –
His Sea in no wonder the same -
  his Sea and the same through each wonder:
  His Sea as she rages or stills?
So and no otherwise – so and no otherwise –
  hillmen desire their Hills.

Who hath desired the Sea?
        Her menaces swift as her mercies?
The in-rolling walls of the fog
        and the silver-winged breeze that disperses?
The unstable mined berg going South
        and the calvings and groans that declare it –
White water half-guessed overside
        and the moon breaking timely to bare it –
His Sea as his fathers have dared –
        his Sea as his children shall dare it:
        His Sea as she serves him or kills?
So and no otherwise – so and no otherwise –
        hillmen desire their Hills.

Who hath desired the Sea?
        Her excellent loneliness rather
Than forecourts of kings, and her outermost
        pits than the streets where men gather
Inland, among dust, under trees –
        inland where the slayer may slay him –
Inland, out of reach of her arms,
        and the bosom whereon he must lay him -
His Sea from the first that betrayed –
        at the last that shall never betray him:
        His Sea that his being fulfils?
So and no otherwise – so and no otherwise –
        hillmen desire their Hills.

Introduction:
Places

My home is the Rocky Mountains. Not in them. All of them. Every place I have ever been, and, I am sure, every place I have not (yet) been, is different, unique. Every one of them has some feature, some characteristic, that appears nowhere else. And yet, each new place, each place I visit for the first time, invariably looks familiar, vaguely familiar. Vast areas are, of course, similar in general to many others, but each small area, a few acres, perhaps a few miles, is similar in detail to places far away, hundreds of miles away. There are parts of the valley of New Mexico's Cimarron River that could be inserted on the road north from Strawberry, Arizona, and their junction could not be detected. Large parts of Arizona's Salt

River Canyon could be transplanted to the Shell Creek Canyon in Wyoming, and the seam could not be perceived. Often, on a new road in a fresh land, I feel an uncertain aquaintance, an indistinct intimacy, a *deja vu*, almost unreal, almost real. I know the land, though I have never before been there. There is another place, a place I was happy, a place close to my soul, far, far away, and yet, it is here. The spirit of that place and time is the spirit of these. Not similar. Identical. It is the same spirit, for Spirit is apart from Space and Time.

Some things are present everywhere. The same sun rises, and though every dawn is different, every one has the same structure, the same skeleton. Each one follows the same plan. It is like the thousands of distinctive ways one can prepare rice and beans, yet at heart, each recipe is only rice, and beans. Every dawn is different, but every dawn is a dawn. And every dusk is likewise the same, and unique. The sun sets. The light fades. Night falls. And the stars appear. The same stars, never changing. The only real difference is that the stars of Arizona and New Mexico are the Winter stars, and the stars of Montana and Idaho are the Summer stars. But that is only because I have changed, for I winter in the South and summer in the North. The sky is always the same, always an immutable part of every place I love. I look at the stars every night the clouds allow. Sometimes the sky calls, and I watch the stars for hours. Sometimes I find a story there, or a song. Always I wish to fly among them, as if they are my true home, as if I belong there. As if I am a part of them, or they are a part of me. Wherever I go, there I am, and so are the stars. They show me where I am, and when. They show me how to go to new places, unexplored places, the kind of places I treasure. I have never been there, but I know the way.

I am often alone, but usually, there is someone, old friends, gold friends, to share, to enjoy the world. Some of you reading this are gold friends. Come, go with me! Wander the woods, and embrace the exotic till exotic becomes normal. Meet me by chance or intent. Share the wonders of the high montane. Camping at nine thousand feet is like living in mid-air. Hiking the mountain trails, the cliffs and high passes, is like flying, not walking, and your feet become wings.

Gold is a valuable thing, but not at all rare. Large concentrations are rare, but gold itself is everywhere. There is more gold dissolved in the ocean than Man has ever mined. There are traces in all of the soil everywhere in the world. It is there, always. You just have to look for it, and know how to find it. It is the same with old friends. I have tens, hundreds of thousands of old friends. I have only met a few hundred, perhaps a thousand of them, but they are out there. Just like gold, for that is what they are. When I first meet an old friend, I have found gold. Gold friends. I know them as old friends because they are familiar, just like the places. There is Ray at Rueters, in Wyoming. There is Dale at La Posa, in Arizona. They are as similar, and as different, as Salt River and Shell Creek. We share likes and dislikes, ambitions and desires, attitudes and viewpoints. Not all of them, for we have great differences as well, but that is what makes them valuable, and fun. We learn from each other, and we share. It is more fun to share, for in sharing a thing, you double it, and that makes life becomes worthwhile. Beautiful countryside, an environment full of life and joy, glorious skies and infinite stars, these are the elements of Paradise. And when you add old friends, *gold* friends, friends with whom you can share the fun, then you have Heaven, Heaven on Earth. It just does not get any better.

This is the enchantment of wandering. Right over there, on the far side of that hill, is a new place, with new horizons. It is part Heaven, part Space, part Gold Friends. It is *my* place. It lies in a million locations, on mountains and deserts, in valleys and canyons, by rivers and lakes, everywhere. It encompasses, at the very least, all of the Rocky Mountains. Each new place can be experienced for a weekend, or inhabited for ever, at your choice. A very few of these places, my places, are described in this book. You can just visit, but I plan to stay. Perhaps we will meet there, in every place that I have ever been, and in every place that I have not yet been.

Because I'm going to go back there, some day.

The Magic Door

It is really not that surprising, when one comes to think of it. It is logical, it makes sense. The only peculiarity is that it would take so long to notice it, to become aware of it. For most people, it would be very unusual. It certainly was for Dorothy; once the twister had passed, she arose from her bed, made her way through the familiar furniture, and opened the front door on a completely new and different world. Of course she was surprised; you would be, too. Imagine: You live in a house, or perhaps an apartment, where you have lived for some time, months at least, preferably years, or even all of your life. Everything is familiar and where it is accustomed to be, and the view from the front door is as well known to you as the arrangement of the furniture in your bedroom. You get up in the morning, and all is normal. You walk through the house, and all is normal. You open the front door and . . . where am I? Instead of the apartment building hallway, you face a Victorian garden.   Instead of the familiar neighborhood, you see a tropical jungle. Instead of the Kansas farm, you see Oz.

I live in a tent, designed specifically for my needs and comforts and preferences. To one side I place my cot. To the other I place my bags of clothing and laundry, my box of snacks (fruits and cookies and crackers and such), my books and computer and notebook, my cigarette makin's. Everything has its accustomed place, ready to hand, right where I know to look for it. Everywhere I go, I pitch it and furnish it in exactly the same way. The door even faces as close to East as I can arrange. If you were to sit inside my tent with the curtains down and the door sealed shut, you would have virtually no clue to where the camp was. If you are sufficiently familiar with the voices of trees, you might guess that you were in a forest, and even what kind of forest. You might hear a babbling brook or the sound of surf, and realize there was a body of water nearby. You might even hear childish laughter or the grumble of a generator, though my day usually begins before such sounds do, and know you were in a campground. But what would you see when you opened the door?

Yesterday I opened the door to a world of grays and tans, to pristinely clear and still desert air, arid sand and stands of stunted brush. A roadrunner and a pair of jackrabbits paused to decide whether I was a threat or not. The sun was just breaking the horizon, and its brilliant beam drew a shining line across the surface of a lake. There was no sound, none at all. Today, the world beyond the door is green and brown. There is coarse gravel at my feet (common to many campgrounds), giving way to a stretch of brown duff, with spring grasses sprouting among tall junipers and taller live oaks. A doe, wary but not startled, eyes me from the semi-shade. Sunlight breaking through the leafy branches draws lines in the air, perfectly straight and parallel, though from my viewpoint they spread in a sacred star pattern, clear and precise in the uniform pall of smoke from a distant forest fire. In a week or so, I shall emerge to a thick forest of ancient ponderosa pines, deep in a dell with walls so steep, the first rays of morning sun do not strike till halfway to noon. Later I shall camp near the lip of a cliff and, lying below me, a green valley fifty or sixty miles long, perhaps clear all the way to the horizon, perhaps fading to nothing in thin morning mist. Or, perhaps, filled with low clouds, blindingly bright in the light of the sun, solitary in a sky of unbroken blue, with no sight of land save the rock on which I stand.

At times like these, I could almost wish I was a drinking man, so I could awake, bleary and befuddled, with no recall of where I am, and no idea what lies on the other side of the Door. Even so, there are times when I can approach such wonder. The vagaries of weather may have me emerge inside a cloud, a fog-like stillness where objects barely thirty feet away are blurred, and beyond fifty feet are so insubstantial, I can not be sure they are there at all. Or rain may darken and dim all objects to a dreary gray, in a soaked silence as if the water had washed all sound away. Once, on a cold July morning at ten thousand feet, the brilliant green land on which the sun had set was gone, replaced by a blanket of glistening fresh snow.

Occam's Razor is a principle of science which states that, when there are several possible answers to a question, the simplest of them is most likely to be correct. There are many possible explanations for this phenomenon I have described. It could be change of location, but sometimes, as in the snowfall, location has not changed. It could be change of weather, but sometimes, such as last night, the weather is the same. It could be a man-made factor, such as the midnight arrival of a motor home or a troop of travelers who made their camp just east of mine, or a controlled fire far upwind, dispelling accumulated fire-load and instilling the air with misty white smoke. Any of these could explain some instances, but it requires all of them together, and more, to account for every occurrence. There is another explanation, a simple one, that could, alone, create every change of view I have ever experienced, and more. It is unlikely. Some would say it is impossible, even absurd, but some said the same about flying machines, and I am fairly sure *they* exist. I do not really know, and I cannot say with absolute certainty that this is fact, but it *is* the simplest solution.

You see, it is the Door. It is Magic.

El Vado Lake

New Mexico

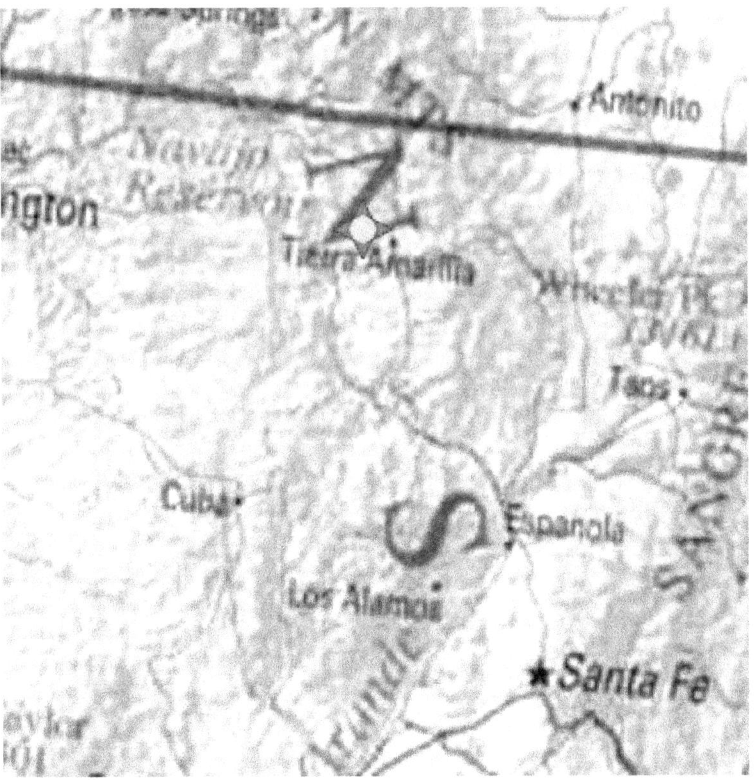

The Mesa

Few people would fail to recognize a mesa. Everyone knows its appearance. It is smaller than a mountain, larger than a hill, a stone table, flat on the top, sides as vertical as rainfall, the lower half or third or quarter a talus slope, halfway between horizontal and vertical, and as flat as flat can ever be. The rock is brown and yellow and red, and if there is any vegetation, it is rare, and as brown and sere as the broken stone, invisible from enough distance to see the mesa for what it is. That is Mesa, desert mountain.

This is a mesa that does not dwell in the desert. It stands in a forest, its shed stone tumbling to a lake. It lies buried in its own talus, barely a tithe of cliff standing bold above it. The top is as flat as we all know it should be, but it bears a forest of pines and junipers, a table whose centerpiece has run wild, ambitious to be a tablecloth, even hanging over the edge, securing the slopes, holding erosion at bay, concealing the cliffs and maintaining the mass of the mountain for future generations. The scant stretch of bare cliff bears traditional colors, cream and beige, tan, brown, faded and bland in the dawn shadow, flashing as fire when sunlight strikes, yellow and orange and hot, hot white. As sunlight descends the forested fall, the trees arise in their fall raiment, greens ands browns, and red, yellow, orange, a blaze of glory exceeding even New England Autumn.

No mist arises from the lake today. No haze dulls the colors or softens the sharp shadows. The focus is so fine, one can see the strata in the climbing flora, a band of cottonwood along the shore, alternating deep green and black shadow as conical conifers climb up the first incline, then bold bands, horizontal sweeps, impressionist brushstrokes of green, the same hue as below and above, but seeming brighter for the absence of shadow. The horizontal scheme collides and blends with the descending vertical as a muddy river debouches into the sea, gullies and landslips and paths of rolling rocks reach from the cliffs to the clinging forest. Steeper slopes bear fewer trees, for the soil is thinner, and the questing roots find less to grip. Lesser life, the grass and the brush, lay claim to the land, and proclaim it with their colors, tawny and russet, cross-hatching the ledges and gullies with their stairs and stripes, their red white and brown tri-color. And here, and there, scattered scouts or pioneers, interlopers or romantic fools, adventurous pines invade the domain of the little people, striving to survive where the wise woods dare not grow. These are the outcasts, the scattered seed fallen from the pines of the plateau, of the highborn, lower than their sires, but still holding themselves above the rubble below, though forever cut off from their forebears by the cliff, towering twice as tall as the trees can ever hope to be.

The cliff is a bastion, a curtain wall, a castle keep that forever separates the elite above from the barbarians below. No, not forever; the talus scaling ladders strive to bury the battlements, and at one point, only one, have succeeded, and the pine regiments flow from the cottonwood seige lines, smoothly, unbroken, through the breach, merging with the crenellations of tree-tops against the sky.

The cliff is a dam, creating a wooden lake, a mirror to the water that reflects it below, mirrors within mirrors, one bearing flocks of fish, the other, schools of birds. And through the breach in the dam flows a treefall, descending in its infinite slowness to the pine pools beneath, brown brush foam breaking around a protruding crag and limning the base where the waters of the lake form the banks of the pine pool. Salmon-swallows and herring-wrens and trout-robins work their way up the rootbound rapids, flitting from branch to branch, upward, upward, to crest the ridge and happily rest at last in sylvan serenity, on top of the world.

This is a mesa like all other mesas, unique, distinct, disparate. It is solid, tangible, a rock. It is fantastic, magical, ethereal. It is immutable and ever-changing. It is what it is, and whatever you want it to be. All you have to do is look, and add one teaspoon of imagination.

Eternity

I sit in the shade on the shore of a lake. Before me lies the water, breeze-ruffled nearby, but perfect and smooth by the farther shore, mirroring the mesas that rise beyond, the talus tree-clad till the bare cliffs emerge to rise the final feet, a barren border emphasizing the flat forest above. I feel the breeze, barely. The grass slightly trembles, the trees stand mute in the live silence. Although I am in a campground, a large one, there is no sound, for I am the only occupant. In the week I have been here, I have seen one boat, exactly one, upon the lake. And now from where I sit, there is no sound, no sight, no sign of Man. Not now.

It is not easy to stay in Now. Memory says this is off-season, and compares it with on-season, when the water is more disturbed by wakes than by wind, when every site is filled, and the park teems with people, with children laughing and dogs barking, with radios playing and motors revving, and the air carries the smells of hot dogs and hamburgers and fire-lighter and sunscreen. Memory seeks to drag me from quiet to chaos. Knowledge says the talus was once cliff, and the far shoreline shows that the lake was once deeper. Those mesas were once connected, the plateaus were once ground level, the strata were once seabed, and this spot where I sit did not exist at all. Knowledge seeks to drag me from Is to Might Be.

But the birds do not see it. This sparrow sees only the seeds she snatches from among the tufts of grass. I am not moving, so I am not a hazard. I will move later, and I did move before, so I will be a hazard, and I once was. But will and was are not now. Now is seeds, and seeds are good. Will and was do not exist. Seeds do, and so does hunger.

The universe pulls me away from Now. Recall of past pain colors our perception and invites timidity and a reluctance to experience. Memory of long-gone glories shadows our view and tempts us to dwell in pleasures long past, in phantoms and vapors that no longer exist, may never have existed, for we edit our memories, and believe the altered editions. Thoughts of things we do not have, pleasures paraded to entice, dangers displayed to dismay, tempt and terrify us to leave the present, to search the past for tools and schemes to alter the future toward temptation and away from terror. Ponder and plan have their place, have value and merit and even necessity, but ponder is remembrance of a present that was, and plan is a hope for a present that may be. Present is now, it only is now, it always is now, and nothing more. And nothing less.

I do not care what day it is, or what time it is, or where I am. It does not matter. It is always today, always now, and I am always here. Here may change, but it is always here. Now is now and nothing else. Now is eternal, and here is eternal. Eternity is not a long period of time, for there is no time in Eternity. It has no beginning, and no end. It simply is. Now.

I sit in the shade on the shore of a lake. Memory says I was here an hour ago. Imagination says I shall be here an hour from now. Neither changes the fact that I am here. Neither changes the lake, nor the reflection that differs from the mesa only in the ripple cast forth by a leaping fish. Both can change, if I see fit to change them. But the Now is, and it alone I cannot change. I can create a new Now. I can toss a rock into the lake, and splash a wave on the farther shore. But that is not Now. It will be, it may be, it will never be, at my pleasure. But it is not Now, and Now is eternal.

I made this Now. I do not say I built the mesa, or dug the lake. I put my viewpoint here, and pointed it in this direction, and that created "here". I can change it simply by turning my head, but I do not. I banish that incipient Here to the infinite hoard of Might-Have-Beens, possibilities that never were and never will be, except in illimitable imagination. I cannot do them all, experience them all. Or perhaps I can, but I do not know how. Not now. But it does not matter, not matter at all.

In some future Now I will make a different Here. I will be outrunning the wind on some open and deserted back highway, straddling my bike, the sunlight on my face, watching the landscape rush by, twisting the land to the left or to the right, rolling the world beneath my tires, as I sit stationary in my personal Here. Or I will stand on a cliff as the bike cools and clicks behind me, spreading before me a vast valley, following a river that winds among meadows and trees, between extinct volcanos and eroding upthrusts, watering a herd of elk so distant they appear smaller than the pebbles at my feet. Far, far away, my brother the hawk circles slowly, my brother because he shares my viewpoint, he occupies the same here, though miles away. And a later Here will lie among tall pines that disperse the rising smoke of a cook-fire, fading into shadow, whispering into silence.

Here will change, and Now will change, Some will be planned, and some will surprise, for I am fond of finding places I have never been or seen. Some will be hoped, and never realized. And it does not matter, not matter at all. Because this is Now, and Now is eternal, and I am perfectly happy, perfectly content, to sit in the shade on the shore of a lake.

Clayton Lake

New Mexico

Prairie Shore

We all know the prairie, even if we have never seen it, except in pictures, or even just our minds. It is vast, and flat, all the way to the horizon so infinitely far away. There are farms, crops, pastures, but not everywhere. There are also grasslands, unmodified, unworked, untouched, open land not waiting for the plow, but supporting masses of life, unimaginable tons of insects, unmeasurable throngs of rodents, uncountable flocks of birds, all dwelling among unlimited acres of grass, swimming in the tan waves of a windswept waterless ocean. We know the mountains just as well, perhaps better, for their romance is commonly expressed. Famous is the man who first stood atop Mount Everest, but who was the first man to cross the Great Plains? We remember the bold men who explored the Rocky Mountains and beyond, but do you know who explored the Great Plains? Did you even realize they had been explored? Lewis and Clark labored up the great rivers and struggled through the mountains to the sea on their far side, but what, if anything, did they do regarding the plains between? We know mountains as clad with trees or topped with snow or barer than the day they were born. We know the bear and deer and elk and moose that swarm in their sylvan slopes, we know the pine and fir, the juniper and birch and aspen that shelter their animal inhabitants. Like the prairie, we know them even if we have never seen them, never known them. And we also know the foothills that border the mountains, the worn remnants of eroded bedrock, sand and soil stripped from the heights by wind and rain and ice and time. But between the mountains and the prairie lie not the foothills, but another land, not forgotten so much as ignored. It lacks the far horizons of flat prairie or of high-rising peaks. It lacks the uniformity of ubiquitous grass or of dominating forest. As the shoreline differs from the land and from the sea, so is this border a thing unique unto itself.

It is not rolling hills; that implies a smoothness, and a regularity. This is too rough, too random. It is not a rough or irregular plain, for it is not nearly flat enough. It is not broken country, like the canyons and ravines, except here and there where an ancient wash is accustomed to carve its niche; not deep enough to be a gulch, yet more than a mere gully. It is not a forest, not even wooded, though there are many trees, even a couple of copses. Only one or two percent of the ground is shaded, but the number of trees still qualifies as many, for the land is large, long miles between any structures or fences, or even roads. It is not prairie or meadow or grassland. It is not a great many things. And it has no name, for no single label fits. It is itself, and it is unique, hundreds of square miles of unique.

The land can not be economically farmed, not even to grow hay. It is too rough, too rocky, not flat at any point. Many crops could be grown, but harvesting them would not be easy, not easy at all. One could pasture cattle here, and in a few of the smoother sections, there are indeed small herds, but there is surely more suitable land not too far away. But the land is not barren, not unfruitful, not a wasteland by any means. (But then, is any land truly waste? Is there any land that has no value, practical or not, no redeeming features, any parcel of which one could honestly say, the world would be better, or at least no worse, if it did not exist?)

Grasses grow here, providing abundant forage and seed for the wildlife. Brush and bush do the same, and trees, and also supply shelter and homes for bird and beast. I see birds of many types, songbirds and turkeys, ravens and roadrunners. I see no squirrels or mice, but I know they are there, for I see the hawks circle, and the coyotes prowl, and I heard the owls last night. I see a deer, a doe, followed by three younglings, more than fawns, not yet yearlings. This too is unique, for I have seen many fawns, often twins, or at least pairs, but never before three following a single doe. Perhaps they are triplets; it is not impossible. More likely one or two are orphans, adopted will-she nill-she. They are not the sleek, svelte fashion-plates most people envision. They are rather fat, and shaggy, rough-coated. Summer is long gone, autumn is advancing, and the animals are prepared for cold and for scant forage. Even so, I doubt they will have to suffer much hardship here. The grass is abundant, and should last all winter, though it may not be very appetizing. Except, of course, that hunger will make almost anything appetizing. And even at an altitude of almost a mile, I doubt the snow will drift so deep as to bury the grass beyond the reach of a hungry herbivore.

It is a beautiful land, and therein lies its only commercial value, for here, on one shore of the lake, lies a campground, a state park. Actually, it is not truly commercial value, for the park does little or nothing to fill the state treasury. It pays for itself, its revenues cover its expenses, thus providing sport and recreation without placing any burden on the taxpayers. This is ideal; the costs are paid only by those who use the service. Would that all government services were similarly funded! And there is an accord, a rightness, a good form of irony (but we lack a word for a desireable irony), that the use of this land is based on its beauty and wildness, and thus dependent on *not* using it. If this park were made too big, if it were developed too far, it would destroy its own reason for existence.

It was not always as it is now.. Nothing was. Long ago, many millions, many tens of millions of years ago, this was mud, thick clay mud. There were giants in those olden days, dinosaurs wandering the flats, feasting on the lush vegetation and on the smaller beasts, some as small as chickens, and likely tasting much the same. They trod upon the clay, mud squishing between their toes, and also miniature mammals who did not dodge quickly enough. Later this was ocean, teeming with life-forms now long extinct, though their giga-great-grandchildren still roam the ancient estates, handed down from father to son for millions of generations. Fish, and turtles and alligators dodged from and competed with other reptiles, and left their bones in the gathering layers of silt and sand. Then the land rose up, and the water drained down. The fish and turtles were relegated to narrow lakes and narrower streams, the grasses and flowering plants arose and claimed all the dry land for their own. The majestic dinosaurs departed, and the lowly mammals took their place. It was a long and bloody battle, those millions of years. The dinosaurs bequeathed their holdings to birds, great birds, bigger than ostriches, carnivores who preyed on the tiny mammals who were enlarging from tiny squirrel-sized scavengers, evolving, growing larger while the birds grew smaller and took to flight. Those were magical times, times of long, slow shape-shifting, when the elephantine birds ate the tiny horses and bears and elephants. And all the while, the ice cracked the cliff, and the wind scoured the stones, and the water dug ditches and washed away the dust.

Now the seabed is almost gone, washed away, washed to sea, bedded again where it once was in ages past, and the ancient mud lies spread once again in the sun, pressed and hardened into solid rock, but still bearing the footprints impressed by the forgotten and newly remembered dinosaurs. Grass is king, and squirrel-sized mammals thrive among the stems. A quart-size bunny nibbles the weeds growing between hadrosaurus toeprints. The elk are the largest creatures, still eaten by the dinosaurs' descendants, though now the birds must wait till the mammals are already dead. Owls ambush mice today, but

who knows what will be tomorrow? In ten or twenty million years, this land may be perfectly flat, or covered in steaming jungle. Man may be gone, to the stars or to the fossil beds, and six-foot sentient mice may raise evolved owls as we raise chickens. Or perhaps it will be barren, arid, nothing but sand and stone and wishes of water. We only know it will be, and it will be different.

The land is not what it was, and is not what it will be. And it is not prairie and it is not mountain. But it is what it is, and it is fantastic, magical, enchanting. It is random and logical, planned and fortuitous. It is balanced and unpredictable, improbable almost to impossibility, and perfect, exactly what it should be. It cannot be improved, for then it would have to be something else, and it is happy to be what it is. There is a spirit of this land, which made and shaped it, or was made and shaped by it, or both. Today, now, I am a part of that spirit. In a week, I will be a part of some other spirit, of some other land. But as long as I remember, I will be part of this place, and it will be part of me. And that will be forever, for I never forget. Not in a million years.

Oasis NMSP

New Mexico

The Dunes

There is a hazard inherent in words, for they are intended to carry a concept or a picture from the speaker to the hearer, but the picture created or recalled by the hearer is rarely identical to that of the speaker, and often quite different. Take the word "dune". Most people, on hearing "dune", will think of the vast bleds of the Sahara Desert, covered with long sinuous waves of sand, gentle slopes on the windward side rising to a serpentine ridge, and abruptly plummeting to the lee, mobile features of a trackless tract, wandering across unmappable terrain, changing their locations every year, or month, some even every week. Endless expanses of sand, with outcrops of sand along rivers of sand, smooth sand, rippled sand, blowing sand, and only sand. No rocks, no trees, no grass, not even a single stem. Some people will think of beach dunes such as those of Cape Cod, rolling hills, small, short, bearing scattered stands of sea grass, shaped and controlled, to a small degree, by fences of wire and wood. Mounds of sand of no particular shape, soft sand, warm and smoothed, holding footprints for barely an instant, but flowing, collapsing, showing that there *was* a print, once, but nothing more. And the next good wind obliterates even that.

These dunes are different. They do not roll, they writhe. Neither constant nor uniform, and yet not random, they slither across the landscape, slopes varying from almost level to seventy and eighty degrees. There is much more grass than bare sand, and no sign of erosion, no immediate sign. There are dips, but no gullies, banks, but no valleys. If enough rain fell to saturate the sand, there would be no runoff. The low places would fill, but the pools would not flow, for every direction is blocked by ridges; there are no streambeds, no wadis or washes, no fans of alluvium, no trace, none, that water has ever flowed.

The secret lies in the sand. You see a stretch of bare dust, smooth, unmarked, and walk across it, and turn, and look. Your tracks are clear, sharp, detailed. If there is writing on your sole, you can read it in the earth. You pick up a handful and ... it is not dust. It *looks* like dust, pale brown, grains too fine to be discerned from farther than six inches away, but it is not. It is sand. Toss a handful in the air. A tiny amount of dust, not a teaspoon in a pint, drifts away on the air. The rest fall like rocks. The grains were not formed by falling water, rubbing rock on rock, but by freezing, fractured by expanding ice. Ice splits cliffs, then splits the resulting monoliths and boulders, rocks, pebbles, gravel, sand. It takes a long time, so very, very long, to split the entirety of a mountain into *nothing* except sand, and longer, much longer, to accomplish such a deed without the aid of flowing streams. Yet here it has been done. Almost all of the dust that ever formed here has blown away, and all of the rocks, *all* of them, are now sand. I have searched, and found not a single pebble.

Sand thus formed is not like beach sand. The surf lifts the sand, shifts it, rubs the grains together, breaking off the sharp points smoothly and polishing and forcing it to conform till the sand takes on the characteristics of water, and flows almost as freely as a liquid. This sand is different. It has not been worn down, not been ground into submission. It is small, but it is fiercely sharp. It will interact and interlock with its neighbors, cling to those around it, stand together and hold its position as a bulldog will hold to a leg. Pick a dune, any dune, and dig. You will build a hole as easily as in clay, easier, for the sand will not cling to the shovel. Dig down eight, nine, ten feet, cutting the sides perfectly straight and square and vertical. Then dig sideways. Dig a tunnel. It can be done. A big tunnel. In the sand. Dry sand, fine sand. With no shoring. Impossible in the Sahara or on the Cape, but here, easily done, and the tunnels can endure for years, for decades. I have seen them, tunnels twenty years old, at least.

On the surface, this is a field of dust, of stunted scrub and undernourished grass. It is riddled with the tunnels and dens of rodents, scratched and scribbled with their spoor and those of quail and dove and rattlesnake and roadrunner. It is a paradise for the coyote, so abundant are the rodents, and so easy they are to dig out.

This is a land that can outlast the mountains, for the mountains wear smaller and shorter each year, but these dunes change and remain as they are. A little dust blows away, but less blows in from elsewhere. The grasses anchor the dunes, but the sand slowly buries the grass. A ridge falls into a hollow, and a new hollow empties beside it. These dunes dance a pavane in the wind, expending a hundred years to accomplish what a Sahara dune will do in one as it twists in the simooms. Time is slower here, for it has worked long, and hard. Days pass slowly, even when one is entranced and having fun. It is a quiet land, laid back, mellow, with a hillbilly attitude. Nothin' is broke, so nothin' needs fixin'. It ain't rainin', so the roof don't leak. And my hammock is already slung, so I might's well go use it.

Brantley Lake

New Mexico

Brantley Lake

When you first arrive at Brantley Lake, you might well wonder why it ranks among my special places. The campground has little to recommend it. It is nice. Most campsites have decent shade, with water, and some with electricity. The lake has pretty good fishing, though the officials recommend you not eat the fish, due to DDT contamination. Rather odd, since DDT has been shown to be not harmful to mammals. Other than that, there is not much here. Near here, well, that is another story.

About fifteen miles south is another state park, the Living Desert Zoo. There is no camping at this park, but it is very conveniently close to Brantley Lake. In the great San Diego Zoo, the animal's enclosures replicate their natural habitat, as far as is feasible. Not here. Here the enclosures *are* the natural habitats, for all of the plant and animal exhibits are of the indigenous species. You could spend weeks wandering the New Mexico deserts, seeking the local wildlife, and maybe, if you are lucky and skillful, finding half of them. But at the Living Desert Zoo, you can spend half a day and see them *all*. Well, maybe not all. Some of them, especially the nocturnals, may not be visible. But there is also a wealth of information, as you would expect of a decent zoo, at each display, and you do not have to walk nearly as far. True, you will miss the openness and vastness of the land, but all things considered, it is a wonderful place. You may want to visit it two or three times during your stay.

Another twenty miles will bring you to Carlsbad Caverns National Park. It is *very* popular, and with good reason. In my opinion, if you could only visit one cave system in your life, this would be the one to choose. You can easily spend an entire day there, and may want to return a couple of times.

These two attractions are enough to justify a visit to Brantley Park; either one on its own would be sufficient. But there is one other: The landscape around the park. At first glance, it is nothing. Just a wasteland. But it is also very special. See the Living Desert Zoo first. Think of it as a field guide. Then read the next essay. Finally, follow the trails from the campground. See the Wild Desert, as it really is.

Wasteland

There are lands that are green and lush, with trees in vast groves, and thick bushes of redolent honeysuckle and appetizing blueberry, and grasses and clover and flowers filling every space they can possibly find between. Lands with cool ponds and singing brooks and quiet lakes, lands copiously crammed with life, with deer and squirrels and bees and frogs. Moist lands, fragrant lands, vibrant and alive, eagerly sought by artists, campers and sporters, indeed, by almost everyone.

There are lands that are fertile, prime croplands that bring forth two, three, even four crops every year, and each a bumper crop. There are pastures that teem with plump cattle, every cow with a calf, every ewe with a lamb, or even two, frolicking with the youthful joy of life, fearless of any danger, for there is none, and nothing to fear. Fat lands, rich lands, true wealth, *real* estate. The treasured dream of every farmer and rancher, and of every seeker for the simple life.

This is not one of those lands. It is arid and barren. It has no soil to speak of, just rock and gravel and sand and dust, nothing organic, nothing to enrich, to fertilize. It is lifeless, or the next thing to it. It displays no value for anyone or any thing. Bland, drab, colorless, cheerless, uninviting. Hostile, hazardous, forbidding, deeply and intensely unpropitious. It is vast stretches of dry emptiness, with only a few hardy weeds struggling to make the best of a land where "best" has no meaning. It is hardly worth a single glance, contains nothing to attract attention or to hold one's interest. It is empty. It is nothing. It has no purpose. It is known as wasteland.

What passes for trees are stunted giants almost three feet tall. Two thirds of their branches are leafless sticks, bare bones that appear dead, and may be, though these water-misers do not waste their scanty hoards of moisture on display, and only produce enough leaves to survive till the hoped-for, but never certain, next rain.

While some appear as miniature trees, esthetic, even beautiful, most are random collections of twisted leafless twigs, destitute, ragged, poverty-stricken indigents, refusing to exert themselves in the slightest way, and waiting, waiting for rain.

Waiting.

And the shrubs are no better. All are scant and scrawny, scattered, solitary. Two plants within a yard of each other would feel crowded. And the grass ... well, there is none.

But farther on, the plants begin to grow more closely together. Not thickly, but close enough that you cannot walk between without touching them. A wall off in the distance, in a valley, or perhaps just a gully, may even be a thicket.

When you reach it, you find the wall is no such thing; there are gaps, small clearings interspersed with clumps of bramble and brush. Indeed, it is the same as the territory you have already crossed, except that there are more plants. They do not increase uniformly, no longer sharing the land equally, but rather gathering together, as if considering the idea of forming groves. The groups grow larger, the clearings smaller, the brush taller, the crowding denser.

Here the first true trees appear, eight feet, ten feet tall, and more. Where up till now, all we have seen are hard and woody plants, softer weeds become suddenly abundant, mullein and fluffy reeds. The clear spaces reluctantly disappear, and the long anticipated wall stands before us.

But it is all dead, even the trees, brown, dry, brittle, naught but a memory, the ruins of a once green hope. Only a single stubborn survivor still bears living leaves. Its presence only emphasizes the bleak and blighted despair of the rest.

But a bit beyond, along a bare trail trampled through the mausoleum thicket, lies further evidence, a level line of foul dessicated scum clinging to the dead branches, proof that once, and not that long ago, water flowed here, water more than six feet deep.

Where once water flowed, there can it flow again. And it will.

For this land of death is not dead. Some is still green; only a small percentage, but even so, it is an appreciable amount. And the remainder, the gray and brown corpses, ahh, they are not dead! They only sleep, waiting for the rains. These are not your soft fatland plants, effete plants requiring their daily drink lest they petulantly shrivel and wither away. These plants are the very epitome of toughness and practicality. They can

sleep long, long, then awake, blossom and seed, and return to sleep in a few days, a week, no more. They can survive, no, they can *thrive*, and they do, lustily. And they do not survive alone.

They share the land with the more commonly known desert flora, the ubiquitous prickly pear cactus, and the tiny desert wildflowers, so small and sparse that most tourists never notice them, not till a rain enables them to carpet the sands with color.

And these plants, the ones that do not sleep, but do gallantly continue to grow, to flourish even when there appears not to be anything to sustain them, yet provide constant sustenance for the fauna. Yes, there are animals here, along with the plants. You have not seen them, have you? They hide well, for there are also predators. But you can see their sign. *Someone* has nibbled on the cactus and the herbs.

They are here. Do you see them?

Of course not. They are hiding. Mice, and jack rabbits, and quail, and horned toads, and lizards, and scorpions, and beetles, and bees, and so on, and on, and on...

But they are hiding. They are very good at hiding. The ones who were not are dead, for there are also hawks, and turkey buzzards, and coyotes, and owls, and rattlesnakes. And men. With guns.

A large part of hiding is just sitting still. If you do not move, then you are harder to see. If you do not move, then you make no sound. If you are not seen and not heard, then, perhaps, you might survive.

Remember this. You, too, can be hard to see. If the animals do not know you are there, they will come out. If you sit still, very still, and remain quiet, utterly silent, the rabbits will hop forth eventually to nibble on the greens, the quail will run through your camp in search of seeds, and the chaparral cock will come to investigate, perhaps hoping for a bit of hot dog or lunchmeat.

But if you make a move or a sound, they will know it. They are also very good at spotting danger. After all, they are still alive, aren't they?

Look again at this land, take a fresh look with new eyes, educated eyes, eyes that, now, have seen a thing or two. It is arid. The soil is poor, rocks and sand. But it is rich with life, hidden life, tough, tenacious, skilled at survival, wise in the technology of making the most of what little is available, building a rich and rewarding existence from almost nothing, prevailing against the odds, and content in the deep satisfaction of a difficult task competently accomplished.

This land is not worth a single glance; it requires a long look, an immersion of the senses, an investment of attention, an investment that will reward you well with opulent dividends of admiration. If you give it only that single glance, and dismiss it as unworthy of attention, then you waste its unique beauty.

Only then, and only for you, is it a wasteland.

Morphy Lake

New Mexico

The Journey In

Morphy Lake is a place to love. It intrigued me from the first day I read the description, a small lake at eighty-five hundred feet. No RVs or trailers over eighteen feet allowed. Such a park just *has* to be fine! Last year I had to give it a miss, as I needed internet access, and so had to stay at Coyote Creek. But while I was there, I made a side trip to Morphy to check it out; it was only twenty seven miles, and it proved to be everything I expected. No electricity, of course, and no showers. The web page said there is water in the park, but I saw none. Except the lake, of course.

This year I made it a point to camp here. I arrived this afternoon, and earned a good stay. The road in is bad. First off, it is narrow. The very beginning, in the town of Ledoux, is so narrow, two cars (let alone two RVs) cannot pass. A car and a bike, even a bike with a trailer, can do it. Barely. One hundred feet of that (and it is steep as well) and the road widens to where two cars can pass, if they take it slowly. In the second place, the road is in poor repair. The edges tend to be undercut, and in many places have calved away a foot or more into the roadway, leaving an abrupt drop of several inches. If a trailer wheel were to drop over such an edge, it could throw the bike. If the bike itself hit it, it would surely fall. And there are potholes in the road, up to (down to?) eight inches deep, some less than a foot across, some over three feet. And they are sociable potholes; I do not recall seeing any alone. They always come in groups, families. One I can dodge, and miss it with both the bike and the trailer tires. But three of them side by side, or six or eight scattered across both lanes, well, it is like a shotgun blast. All I can do is slow down and ease through at five miles per hour, or less. To make it worse, the road is very three-dimensional. It twists and winds as it goes uphill and down (mostly up), so I had to make the whole passage (four miles) in first or second gear. I think I got up to third once, for about two hundred yards. Fortunately there was little traffic. It is daunting for a motorcycle; it is a taste of Hell for a bike and trailer. But I was determined to camp at Morphy Lake. I had no reservation, as all of the sites are First Come First Served, but it was Wednesday, so I was virtually assured a site, No, I would not give up, I would not turn around. In any case, there was not enough room to turn around.

Finally I reached the park There is a big sign by the road, "Warning: Lake Ahead". Good thing, too. The entry road is straight, and steep, and turns off sharply at the bottom. If you do not turn, you are on the boat ramp, and sixty or seventy feet later, you are in the lake. If you take the hill too fast, or your brakes fail, you are going swimming. And the lake is *cold!* This steep stretch of road is paved, mostly. Maybe two-thirds. The rest is potholes, big ones, the ancestors of the ones on the road in. Plus, it is scantily covered in loose gravel, just enough to make traction uncertain. I could see it would be no problem hauling the trailer back up, but getting it down was another story. As luck would have it, I had just suffered through a similar situation on a much smaller scale. I did not know it at the time, but it had been primary training for this road. "Steep Slopes 101". I sincerely hope this slope is not gradient training for a worse one later! Well, I had to take the slope slowly, so slowly I would need both feet on the ground to keep the bike upright. I could not count on reliable traction because of the gravel. I would also not be able to use the rear brake; that requires my right foot, and it was needed on the ground. As I had learned, the front brake is not enough to hold back the trailer. So I did the obvious (obvious to a biker); I killed the motor, switched off the ignition, and used the clutch as a brake. I quite literally inched down the hill, slacking the brakes, then stopping after rolling for only a few inches, less than a foot, never letting momentum build, never letting the speed rise. Over and over, a hundred, two hundred times, till the incline declined to a more level space. I turned right onto level, smooth, gravel-free pavement. *Why* is there gravel on the slope, but not on the level?

I started the moter and began to slowly (first gear only) cruise through the campground. I rejected one site that looked pretty easy to get in to, and flat on top, because it was next to the day-use area. I am told this is a popular fishing spot, and I would just as soon not endure the clamor of a few dozen weekend fishers. The rest of the sites I rejected, one by one, as unusable. Dirt ramps to get to them, steep, and with no flat at the top, or bottom for the ones downhill of the road. In each case, I could see I could get in easily (more or less), or out easily, but not both. Only one looked doable; I could get in using the skills I had just learned entering the campground itself. Getting back out would require unhitching the trailer and positioning it manually, but I would be doing that anyway. I went on, deeper into the park, till the road went up, steeply, and winding left and right at the same time. I could get up, sure, but I do *not* want to lead Old Dan back down. He can get downright persnickety about going downhill. So I turned around. That is another of those "bomb went off" statements. The road is narrow. The downhill side drops off at a thirty degree angle. The uphill side rises at a steeper angle. I have *exactly* the width of the narrow road to back-and-fill. With a trailer. Rule #1 of biking with a trailer: TAKE IT SLOWLY. I did, and it was actually very easy (if tense) and straightforward. I went back to the doable site (#14) and slipped in just as I had envisioned. It was work. It was sweaty. But it got done. It was a job that merited a pint of ice cream as a reward, and fortunately, with my far-sighted wisdom, I had just bought a pint on the way up.

The site is not perfect, but it will do. One end of the tent will be eight inches higher than the other; that is okay. Campfires are not allowed, but the weather is clement, so that is also okay. The campground is not a fifth full, and most of them will leave before dusk. The few campers are kindred souls. The woods are beautiful, the lake is serene, the chipmunks are playful and friendly, and there are even geese in the lake. And fish. Another waterbird, an osprey, I think, is circling over it right now. This site has the best view in the whole park.

The travel here was truly travail But I am here, and it was worth it, and I will do it again next year. Beware, you bikers who want to visit Morphy Lake. (Actually, for a bike with no trailer, it would not be nearly so bad.) But once you get here, you will agree, it *is* worth it. I am staying the full two weeks allowed. It will be glorious!

The One-Eyed Man

A young woman was walking by my camp. She said "Hi". I said "Hello! Isn't it a beautiful lake?" She replied, very indifferently, "I've seen better lakes".

That was all she could say, all she could see, all she could know. I was tempted to tell her that I doubted that, and that I doubted she had ever seen *any* lake, truly *seen* it. Or possibly ever seen *anything*. But she would not have understood. It probably would have made her angry.

Instead, I said it was true, there were many more beautiful lakes, and none as beautiful. Look at the rocks above us, the bones of the earth, the bedrock breaking through, old, cracked, worn, lichen-covered. Every lake, every land, is beautiful in its own way. And there is no lake anywhere that is quite like this one. She shrugged, said they were only rocks, and walked on.

I only have one eye, and it is so myopic, I can only see things that are very near to me. But at least I do see that little, and am aware, or at least have a glimmering, of how much more there is, to see, to feel, to understand, to know. Many people are as blind as that poor girl, not even aware that there is such a thing as sight. They have eyes, they could use them, but first they have to open their eyelids. Why do they not? Are they hypnotized, drugged, canalized by their culture, believing everything they are told, even when these things contradict themselves? Are they so accustomed to being told what they see and hear and feel that they reject everything they perceive for themselves?

Yes, they are, and they do.

First Dawn

I could not resist it. Like a child on Christmas Morn, I was up at a quarter to four. The false dawn was fading, and Jupiter shone reflected in the perfectly still waters of Morphy Lake. The cold mountain air still slept, and not the slightest ripple ruffled the surface. Gradually the stars faded, slowly the trees on the far shore took form, individuals coalescing from the dim mass called Forest. One by one, concentric rings began to blossom as fish began to feed. Colors were born of the dimly lightening sky, greens and reds and browns, for this is no rain forest, no Canadian boreal forest. This is the southern Rocky Mountains, and the soil is shallow, the hillsides are seamed with bedrock and cliffs, and with the scars of old fires and landslides. The further ridges glow first, then the rising sun tinges the tops of the trees.

The first breeze lightly caresses the lake, and she shivers in ecstatic response. The perfectly reflected trees tremble and blur, and dissolve into broad impressionist strokes of color, barring the lake, revealing her for what she is. Sets of circles compete with ruled ripples as fish slurp down floating insects, and leap to snap up those still flying. In the shallows an erratic line furrows the surface as a fish pursues a minnow. The tracks of the wind scar the surface, bands of silver separating areas shadowed from the air currents. The wind dies, the waters slowly smooth. Reflections return and gradually regain focus. A small fish skitters into the air, attempting to elude a predator, and succeeds, for an osprey strikes, and the predator finds a meal, but only by becoming one.

All is still and silent save for the splashes from the lake. Yet what feverish activity those splashes denote, the merest fringes of the frenzy of morning feeding. The first direct sunlight falls upon the lake, and the lake glistens in response. The songbirds awake, and flit to the shores to drink. Their throats wetted, they burst into morning song, celebrating my first dawn at Morphy Lake.

Good Morning!

The Lake

It is not much of a lake. No, that is not right. It is a *small* lake. I have known ponds in New England that were larger. But this is the West. The land is larger, the trees are larger, the hills are larger, the very sky itself is larger. Everything is larger than Back East, everything except the water. Lakes are the size of ponds, rivers are the size of creeks, at least when they are not altogether dry. I once stepped across the Rio Grande. The name means "Big River". One step. Did not even get a foot wet. Of course, the next day the river was two hundred feet wide, and raging. The West is like that.

Morphy Lake is small, but still much of a lake. The fish are abundant, and hungry, and sweet. It is a larder for ducks and geese and ospreys, a pair of Great Blue Herons, maybe even eagles, though I have seen none so far. The shore is lined with rich pine forest, and the bowl is surrounded by rings of ridges (usually snow-capped, but there was no snowfall this year), marching off to the horizon. As the lake lies at eighty five hundred feet, the soil is sparse, and bedrock protrudes in many spots. Old bedrock, weathered, worn, chewed by the acid secretions of the lichen that covers some completely, not a pebble of rock being visible. And the trees are not too thickly set. The forest is healthy. Wildfire simply passes through, devouring the fallen branches, killing seedlings, thinning saplings, but only warming the tall trees. The setting is perfect for this jewel of a lake.

Yes, it is small, barely a thousand feet in its longest dimension, and growing smaller. The water level was once ten feet higher than it is today. But that is normal. In the East, it rains very much; in the West, it rains every year. Usually. One never knows what one will get. But this is May. July and August may be wet, soaked, saturated. That is the normal pattern. Come September, this lake may be brim full and overflowing. If not this year, then the next, or the next, or eventually. Of *that* you may be certain.

Meanwhile, there is water enough. At least, the fish have made no complaints. Quite the contrary, in fact. When they are caught, they make very pointed and barbed comments on the lack of water up here, and request that you put them back in the lake, thank you kindly. And many of the fishers do put them back. Me, I keep them. I do not fish for the fun of it, though it is fun. I fish for food. You simply cannot buy fish as good as these, for even if you find a store that stocks them live, they insist on killing the fish before you can take them, and by the time you get them home, they are no longer truly fresh. For the best fish, you must have it frying within a few minutes of killing it. No, I fish for food. I actually resent catching fish, in a way. Here I am, sitting, very relaxed, in a boat or on the shore, immersing myself in the environment. I am completely at peace, and fully content, when this fish comes along and gobbles my bait, *my* bait, grabs on to the hook, and starts running away with it. I have to haul him in and pull the hook out, getting my hands all slimy and stinky, and usually replace the bait, before I can return to my placid contemplation of the surroundings. That ill-mannered intruder *deserves* to be eaten!

But the fishing here truly is good. The lake is stocked frequently (New Mexico is very serious about fish stocking), so it is a very popular site for fishing. Or perhaps it is stocked *because* it is so popular. Here it is, a Thursday morning in early May, not two hours after dawn, and there are a dozen fishers on the shore, and five or six more in boats. Imagine what it will be like come Saturday! Standing Room Only, no doubt.

The boat rules are good, too. It being a rather small lake, there is no sense in using much of a motor, so boaters are restricted to oars or electric. Quiet. The whole place is quiet. Cars are rare, and when they do come, they do not run long. Fishers are quiet people. In fact, the greatest amount of sound is the calls of the ravens. Even the wind is more silent; there is very little of it, mostly soft breezes. There may be a constant roar endemic in the waters, but above the lake itself, peace prevails. At least on the surface.

The Rocks

The hill is a rock, a single solid mass of ancient granite. Its face has been painted, as that of a lady of fashion, its powder and rouge being soil and stones, and pines and their duff, and pinecones and even a little grass. A few campsite beauty marks have been added.

Little of the true hill can be seen, or perhaps much, for the protruding masses and ridges look much like the separated slabs and shivered stones that slip with greater-than-glacial slowness down to, ultimately, the sea.

Each rock is uniquely the same, gray, and green with lichen, and black with mold, split and cracked and carved by ice and roots, tumbled and jarred against its brethren, shattered and ground into cobble and shingle and pebbles and gravel, inevitably into sand, soil, dust. The rock is gray, but the soil born of it is brown. Perhaps it has partaken of the color of the duff, the bleached brown of decaying pine needles. A few, a very few, rocks of white or red or brown inhabit the hillside, immigrants, intruders, foreigners, imported by Man, who made this campground, as well as the small lake which gives the campground both its name and it reason for being. Both the campground and the lake are as artificial as a birds nest, made by arts for a specific purpose, but the hill and its hillside are not. They are as we found them, as they would be had we never come. As they have been for untold time.

They are old, these rocks, seeming to predate even the bones of Vedauwoo, and rocks simply do not come any older, not on this planet. But the greater age is only a seeming, a glamour. The beauties I admired when I was a youth have aged, some into crones worthy of the bitterest fairy tale, but others into mature matriarchs still attractive, still desireable, still having a beauty that refuses to fade. The matriarchs are in Vedauwoo; these stones here are the crones. Their faces are fractured and pitted, broken and blemished with lichen-spite, and yet, their hideousness holds an unaccountable beauty. Rather than the sameness of a sixteen-year-old's glow, they reveal the experience and character of the living rock. They are Nature's version of Rodin's "Heaulmiêre". The weaker and softer parts have eroded, leaving legacy-lines of sights unseen for these past millions of years, of events that transpired over ages of ice, though no glacier ever ground these faces beneath its feet. Only time and its minions have worked their will, cracking the cliff, then smoothing the sharp edges. Eldritch shapes beckon to the imagination and invite the fantasies to form and embrace the mind. But above all else, beneath and beyond fancy and fact, it is what it is: It is a field of rocks, a random array sculpted to the designs of Chance. The lines and shapes flow and blend and jar with a fitness and a rightness, a canvas, a foundation, a setting, for the beauty which resides in the beholding mind. For that is the true source. Others, bearers of stunted and stultified imaginations, see only rocks, if that much. But if you have a free and open sense of wonder, cast it upon this random array, and you will see. There is no landscape more beautiful. At least, not in the World.

The Wind

What kind of wind can you expect at Morphy Lake? Well, yes and no. I am aware that this answer makes no sense to you. Spend a day there, and it will. This morning at dawn, there was no wind, not a puff, not a breath, none. From Aeolus to Zephyr, it was absent. The lake was literally as smooth as glass. It had been calm all night, and the calm continued till the sunlight touched the waters. Then a breeze started as the slightest hint, enough to affect the water, but not quite enough to feel. It gently touched my cheek, and ran itself through my hair. Slowly it strengthened, till a little after noon, it neared twenty miles per hour.

But that is not accurate. It is true enough, but incomplete. It paints a picture like that of a swift brook, or a rock rolling downhill, gathering momentum, steadily gaining speed. This wind is more like a long series of short falls into an otherwise still pool, or perhaps a Slinky inchworming its way down a staircase. For the wind rises swiftly to a noisy peak, starting with an unfelt whisper in the distance, rising in tone, volume, intensity and nearness. It touches your skin, tickles, caresses, massages and slaps with an eye-watering, hat-flinging force. Loose leaves and dust surge up and flee before the gust.

Then it stops. It does not ease or taper off, or only barely so. It stops. Switched off. Gone. Only the rushing sound remains, and it dwindles rapidly in the distance. For twenty seconds, thirty, a minute, or even two or three, there is nothing but silence. Then the whisper re-sounds, soft, light, far off, but rapidly approaching. It heralds the wind's return, and soon the grass is vibrating, the saplings begin waving, the trees start to sway. It may peak at a tenth of its prior force, or carry on to a new high, or pause at any point between. It may blow for three or four minutes, steady and firm, or it may persist for only ten seconds. Then, again, it stops, and the susurrus disappears over the horizon. There is no predicting it, not accurately. The wind will rise and fade, and the intervals will be as still as an interior room. Beyond that, one cannot know.

The lake responds to the capricious air. The unblemished smooth surface of the dawn is now rough and uneven. Over a distance of only a thousand feet, the wind has raised waves of two to three inches. They break upon the lakeshore with an audible splashing, and roil the water, stirring it to mud-brown, encroaching six or eight feet into the normal muted blue-green. The waves roll on, even when there is no wind. Many minutes were required to build up the rolling wavelets; they will not subside any sooner. Ah, but the wind will not desist that long. The wind scuffs the surface to a dull matte texture, reflecting color, but no shapes. But when the wind dies, when the air is again still, the surface tension of the water instantly smooths the tiny imperfections and restores the pre-dawn mirror finish. It is a poor mirror now, suitable only for a fun-house, for the greater waves resist, and buckle and ripple the reflected images into grotesque caricatures. But the images are there, blurred, misshapen, but recognizable nonetheless.

Sunlight dances upon the water. In a flat calm, it would be a single eye-searing disk, but even when there is no breeze, it is not flat. In the wind-ruffled water it appears as a broad white band that stretches from shore to shore. The distorted mirror of the calm bears a galaxy of flashing, twinkling stars, not sharp pinpoint stars as we see them, but swirling globular stars such as Van Gogh depicted in "Starry Night". The wind erases the display, smearing the light into an amorphous blob; the calm restores the individuality. It is very like a galaxy, with a milky core, the discernable discrete stars, thickly clustered, and thinning, diminishing with distance, dwindling to random sparks on the far side of this aquatic universe. And this pattern is unique; it lasts for a time so minute, even a mayfly would think it short. Then it is gone, but gone to be instantly replaced by a new pattern, equally ephemeral, and another, and another, all the day long. Thus is it unique in time, but also in space, for only I can see it. You, a mere three feet away, observe it at a different angle Only slightly different, only a few seconds of arc, but enough to change the pattern, to lose half of the stars, but to gain an equal number of different ones.

This is what the wind provides at Morphy Lake. It is an orchestra of sound, a chorus of trees singing in the wind, as they dance a slow pavane of pines, counterpointing the waltz of waters and the rhumba of reflections. Ever changing, swelling and fading, always unique, persisting or not, all at once, all day long. Infinite variety, always the same.

This is the kind of wind one should expect here, but it may not be present, and it will, I guarantee, be different.

Fishing

That is the main attraction of Morphy Lake. Most people arrive early or mid-morning and depart mid- or late afternoon, and spend all of their time – all of it – on the shore or in a boat. Fishing. A few stay overnight or for the weekend. Even they spend all day at the water, fishing. They will take their meals at the camp, or perhaps their women-folk will bring lunch down to them. Unless, of course, the women-folk are also fishing, as they often are. They do not hike. Granted, there are no hiking trails at this park. No official ones. You can stroll along the road through the middle of the campground, or pick your way along the shoreline, or walk the length of the fence that surrounds the park. Three very nice, and extremely different, unofficial hiking trails. But only I, and a few kids, and some dogs walking their "masters", use them.

There is nothing wrong with fishing. These people are obviously very fond of it. They invest a fair bit of time, trouble and tender in their day-trips and weekends, just to fish. It gives them a welcome break from their wonted tedium, a chance to relax in the fresh (though thin) air, and even get in a bit of exercise. Not a lot of exercise, the air being, as I said, thin. Near nine thousand feet elevation. And they accomplish something, as well: They catch fresh fish for their dinners. I fish myself, sometimes, though not for sport. If I can catch three or four fish in ten minutes, I am perfectly happy. I love fresh fish, truly fresh, but the only way I can get it is directly and immediately from the lakes and streams. The sooner the fresh fish is in the hot fat, or pinned to the plank, or impaled on the spit, the sooner the fish is cooking after it dies, the better the flavor. Even an hour delay will degrade the taste. I have eaten plenty of fish in the ten days I have been here, but I have yet to catch one. You see, the children have so much fun catching the fish, and there is a plenitude to catch, as the lake is well and frequently stocked. An eager kid goes out in the early morning, and in half an hour has caught his bag limit. He can practice catch-and-release, but the fish are so hungry (the lake being over-populated) they often swallow the hook. They know you should not release a fish that has a hook gouging his stomach. So the family has fish for breakfast, and then he can catch some more. Soon he again has a full bag, and the fun is over for the day. But wait! He has a brilliant idea! "Hey, mister, do you want some fish?" Now I have the limit on *my* license, and brunch, and he gets a fresh start. Everyone wins. Except the fish, but at least they are no longer hungry.

Many people bring their dogs. It is a fun change for them. Instead of spending the day sleeping on the carpet, they get to spend it sleeping on the shore. I do not suppose they mind. One man spent the day in his boat, drifting around, while his big black dog sat in the bow looking around. Never moved much, just looked. But then there is this party down here, with three big dogs, some kind of retriever mix. They spend half of their time romping in the water, and the other half shaking off and rolling in the dirt. Probably scaring the fish, but there are so many, and so hungry, I doubt it matters to the fishers.

The fishers are happy with their recreation, for that is exactly what it is, re-creation, creating anew. They leave here tired but re-freshed, happy to have had a break in their routines, ready, if perhaps a bit unwilling, to resume their day-to-day activities, usually not what they would prefer to do, but quite necessary to feed their families and pay their bills. Here they have created again the life they *want* to live. How fortunate that they can, that places such as this exist, that they are easily accessible, and that people can afford the time and money to use them, and that our government is not so restrictive as to prohibit it. Indeed, most such places are provided, stocked and maintained by the governments.

Savings are supposed to be good for the economy. If this is so, then I am doing a public service. I talk with many people out here, since I love to talk, and the people are so interesting. Among many other things, we discuss this lifestyle, living in these places all year 'round. And many of these friends start cutting expenses and saving money, so that when their children are grown and on their own, these folk can cut loose and live as I do (though doubtless in very different styles), free, to do as they please, with no time pressure, and all of the time in the world.

It is a lot like fishing.

Timing

I am so lucky, and so grateful for it. I came to Morphy Lake at just the right time. Fire danger is extreme, and the Red Flag is out, so no campfires are allowed, at all. However, gathering firewood is not allowed in the park, and there is nowhere to go for miles around to gather it anyway, so the ban is really of no importance, as it would be if I were camping in, say, a National Forest. The kids are still in school, and few people vacation in May, so except for weekends, I pretty much have the place to myself.

The weather is just turning. The last frost is past. The aspens and bushes were pretty much bare when I arrived, a few buds, perhaps, but little else. Now the aspens are all aleaf and dance in the wind, and the bushes are bright green with new growth. Half of the chipmunks were gravid and fat, and now they are thin, in the rare times I see them, when they are not nursing their young The temperature are benign, from the high forties at dawn to seventies in the midafternoon; my neighbors say Albequerque is sweltering.

The dam is to be rebuilt in August, but draining the lake had not begun till the day I arrived. Now the lake drops nearly a foot each day, and the exposed aquatic plants tinge the air with the sweet smell of decay often mis-called the smell of the sea, or of water.

And the weather is changing again. Hotter, drier. School is about to let out for the Summer.

Time to move on. But I will be back.

Cimarron
Canyon

New Mexico

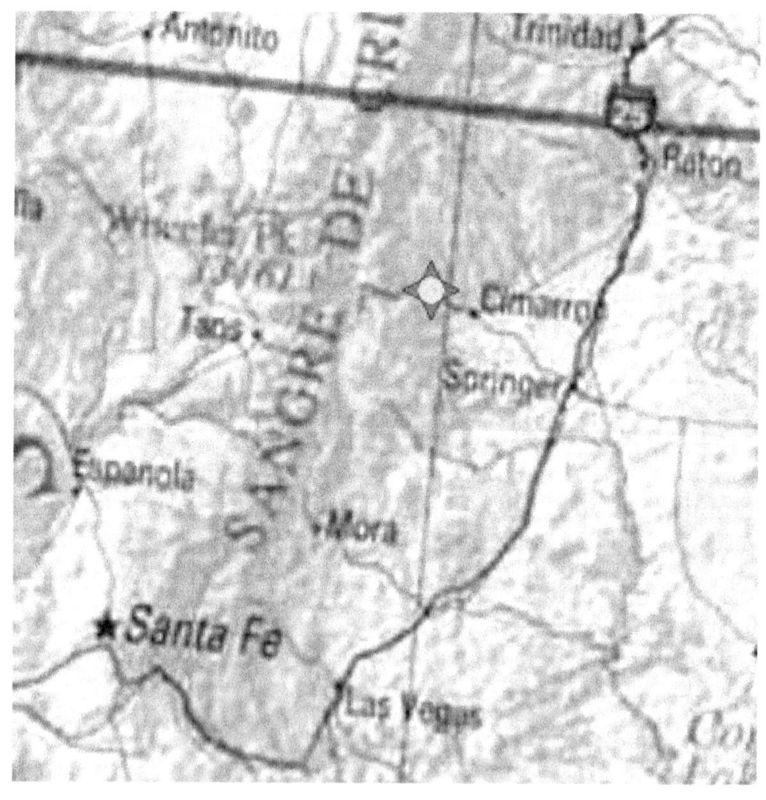

Cimarron Canyon

I arrived in Cimarron Canyon State Park in the early afternoon There were three First Come First Served sites open, all at the same place. One looked almost ideal: Water point right there, toilets nearby. No showers, no electricity, but shady places to sit, all day. The camp host assured me that no campgrounds in the park had showers or electricity, so I paid for this one till Monday. All of the sites adjacent to the river are reservable. Site 2 is the best of them. However, site 18 is almost as good, on the very edge, and almost isolated. Not *quite* as close to water, but the toilets are no farther away.

I loafed for the afternoon, explored the near area, stopped in the Visitor Center for maps and local data. While waiting for evening cool, I started writing. Before I had finished one essay, I had the idea for another. There is something about the spirit of this place that is inspirational. But it was time to pitch the tent, so I desisted and got on with my chores.

The next two days were devoted to exploring. I visited the other three campgrounds in the park. Maverick was cramped, and the Ponderosa was only suitable for big RVs. Blackjack, though, was nearly ideal. Vault toilets instead of flush, such as Tolby has, and no waterpoints, but the Cimarron River is right there, easily accessible, and I have a purifier. The only flaws are the nearness of the highway, and the fact that one must park in the parking lot, then carry your gear in. That can be a couple of hundred yards, depending on which site you select. But the sites are far apart, and there are many, many trees. And no generators, ever. Thunderstorms in the afternoon.

Saturday I went to Angel Fire. I figured the road workers would be off, so I would not have another half-hour wait, or two, as had been inflicted on me on the way in. But the work was done. The whole stretch was completed, and the crew would not be back. I stopped off at Eagle Nest State Park. It is not listed as having camping, but I had been told it had recently been added, and sure enough, the entry signs now have the tent symbol that means camping. It was only one third full, but not impressive. Built on a low marshy area, ramps that look like railroad embankments provide a place to park an RV, and a raised area for a ramada. No place suitable for a tent. I cruised on to the Viet-Nam Veterans Memorial. It is the only state park with no fees. Its chapel never closes. *Never.* Not much to see except a Huey, till you get to the museum in the Visitor Center. Many artifacts of both sides, tools, weapons, clothing, for this memorial is for the Viet Cong as well as for the Americans, and that is as it should be.

Just as I was leaving the memorial, the lights went out. Lightning had struck somewhere. But my luck was holding, because, while the Visitor Center had to be closed when the power was off, I was finished there. I went on to Angel Fire for food, but the power was still off. Black Lake, Red River, Eagle Nest, all blacked out. The store was closed, with an employee turning people away. I suggested he might allow blind people in, which got a good laugh. We had a good party, those of us in no hurry. Half of the people became upset and left. The rest of us chatted and got acquainted and had a fine time. I visited a farmer's market nearby and got the best summer sausage I have ever tasted. After an hour, the power returned, and the party broke up. I finally got my ice cream, and headed back to camp.

By Monday, I had decided to stay another week. There was just too much to see and do, and I had neither schedule nor obligations to meet. It was one of the better decisions of my life, for on Tuesday, Jenny and Laura arrived. Gold friends.

Tolby

New Mexico's Cimarron Canyon State Park comprises four campgrounds. One is Ponderosa, which is basically a parking lot. Wal-Mart with fire rings and outhouses, and no store. It has water hookups and picnic tables, and nothing else. It is a place to park your rig while you explore the area. At one end is a tenting area, basically a space set aside for tents, but you have to lug your gear from the parking lot. Another is Maverick, a couple of dozen sites among trees by a lake. Water, toilets, tables and fire rings. Rather nice, but cramped, with little space between sites. Then there is Blackjack, strictly a tenting area. There is a small parking lot for your car or bike, but no trailers or motor homes. You park your vehicle, then carry your gear to the actual camping area. It has tables and fire rings, outhouses and spaces for tents, well spread out among large trees, and most right by the river. No water except the river, which is fine if you have a water purifier. It is very nice, very quiet, but not mentioned in the park brochures or website. You have to know it is there, or be observant enough to see the sign by the road.

The fourth one is Tolby, a truly beautiful place. The entire campground is planted in a large grove of longleaf cottonwood, old trees, *big* trees. Several ponderosa pines are intermingled with the cottonwoods, so there is plenty of shade. Two-thirds of the ground is not shaded, but there is always a shady spot within a few feet where you can plunk down a chair for a quiet loaf.

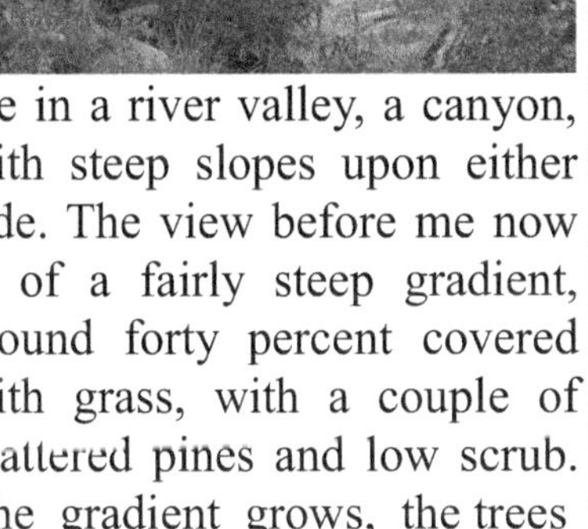

The Cimarron River runs beside the camp. Alas, every one of the campsites on the bank is a reservation site. And there is a highway on the other side, but only lightly travelled. This means, of course, that we are in a river valley, a canyon, with steep slopes upon either side. The view before me now is of a fairly steep gradient, around forty percent covered with grass, with a couple of scattered pines and low scrub. The gradient grows, the trees and bushes thicken till the grass gives up, and the ponderosa covers everything except the outcrops of bare rock, right up to the ridgeline, where the last light of day gilds the highest trees.

Night falls. The birds sing their traditional evening hymn, then retire. The stars come out. Or try to. Alas, less than two hundred feet away, the lights of the toilet building blare into the night and destroy night vision. Even when sitting with my tent between me and the glare it is not enough, for the bright light illuminates the trees before me. I will have to register a formal complaint. A pair of light switches would solve the problem.

Tolby is somewhat contrary. It is the bureaucrats who do it. You see, the campground is in a protected area, so there are limits on what the Park Service can do. There is a power line into the campground, for the toilets and the visitor center, but installing electric outlets for the campsites is not allowed. There are flush toilets and sinks, and a gray water dump station, and therefor septic tanks, but no showers. One of the rangers told me that they (the rangers) had extended the water points. These had existed at one end of the campground. The needed pipe and fittings were on hand, so the rangers went ahead and ran the water lines to the other end and added a half dozen spigots. And promptly got in trouble because there had been no archaeologist on hand to make sure no artifacts were disturbed. In a place where they had already put in a paved road and a half dozen structures. And a septic tank. Like they did not already know this was not an old Indian village burial ground. One wonders how the park was allowed in the first place. Probably it was built before the preservation area was declared.

But it is not important. There is drinking water and a place to deposit used food. Room to pitch a tent, and a place for a fire. Bear-proof food lockers. And a view.

Then the dawn arises and bludgeons all of the lights into insignificance. The greenery fades into color, and the birds awake. Venus and a sliver of Luna rise together in the East as the sky blues, and tiny birds perform complex aerobatics while pursuing invisible insects. The river rumbles its morning song (which is the same as its noon, evening and midnight songs). The rising sun blurs in gauzy morning mists and illuminates the northern hillsides, silhouetting the nearby riverside trees. A cool breeze drifts from the South, the cottonwood leaves sway gently. Hummingbirds investigate the new red things on the

table, and the first "early" riscrs begin to stir from their tents and RVs. The tops of the trees beside me glow. The light drips and flows, lower, lower. And at last the sun bursts over the horizon.

From this campground, I can visit three others, and two more state parks, and see if I can find any old friends I have already met. I can hike several maintained trails, and slowly cruise twisty pine-lined roads, and even visit a grocery store for supplies. Especially ice cream. All within fifteen miles.

This is a good place. My sojourn here will not be permanently terminated. I'll be back.

Cottonwoods

Several species of cottonwood are common in the Southwest. You find them in the deserts and the arid areas, lining rivers and streams and dry washes. They are a boon to the desert wanderer, for they are a sign of hope; almost always, where you find a cottonwood, there will be water within twelve feet. Granted, it may be twelve feet straight down, but it will be there. Almost always. In the hills and the mountains, the cottonwood grows primarily along waterways, even along intermittent ones. Even up to eight, perhaps nine thousand feet, even there the cottonwood thrives.

That is where I am now, camped in a grove of longleaf cottonwood. No saplings these, though there are a few little ones, but mature elders, ancients, many of them more than two feet in diameter, three hundred years old at least, gnarled and twisted into commercial uselessness. No one will build a cabin or cut lumber from these trees! The boles bend and curve, their grain swirls and burls, the wood itself is strangely soft, for a hardwood. The trees are hardy. They are tough, and fragile. There is not one that does not bear dead and withered limbs, and stumps of broken branches, clusters of leafless twigs. Some are as much as ninety percent corpse, but still they sustain a dozen clusters of obstinate green, refusing to surrender and succumb as long as the trunk still stands. But the trunk will fail, in time. A score of stumps stand here in mute testimony to the inevitable end all cottonwoods face: the wind. The soft flesh and the gnarled grain must ultimately yield to twisting winds, and snap off, ten, twenty feet above the root, tearing and shattering along their length, the living leaves plummeting to earth, leaving a tall stump with the whole of one side splintered and stripped away.

Here, within a hundred-foot circle, stand five such stumps, and one rare skeleton, dead, bare, but complete, with not a scar. And a sixth stump, snapped short fifteen feet up, the remnants of its upper four-fifths scattered beside it, but still alive, still bearing two surviving limbs, little more than twigs, blithely leafing away as if nothing had happened. Fragile, and tough.

These cottonwoods are inconsistent. They are each rugged (most very rugged) individualists. They will not, can not grow straight, for they twist, they define gnarled. But here is one that defies the rest, for the trunk is straight and true. With twenty such trees, you could build a log cabin, one with no gaps that allow entry to chill drafts. But there is only the one, tall, lonesome, independent. How very odd it is that "straight and uniform" could be seen as unique characteristics!

I once thought upon the philosophies of trees, how the palm practices "leaves as high as possible", and firs believe in "as high as you can and as wide as you can", oaks and chestnuts pursue "grow wider and wider in every direction". The cottonwood clan has a philosophy that is about as random and unregulated as possible. It is, purely, simply, "Whatever". It will bud a new branch at any point along the

trunk. The new limb can grow at any angle, up, out, even down. Leaves sprout wherever they sprout. The tree is not only an anarchist, it is a chaotist. Not only no rulers, but no rules. "Rule One: There are no rules." Do what you can, when you can, and don't let the little things bother you. Or the big things either. Whatever. It works.

I could live with that.

The Little Folk

People flock to the forests to find the wildlife. They seek the fox and deer and elk and moose, they quest for the elusive mountain goat and bighorn sheep, they scan the skies for raptors, for eagle and hawk, and for vultures and condors and turkey buzzards. They wander the woods in search of big game, for that is what most people conceive when they think of wildlife. And that is okay, for it is a fun thing to do. But it is also very limiting.

Did you know that Man is one of the largest creatures in the world? One of the largest that was *ever* in the world? We are giants! Even considering only mammals, for each species you can name that is larger than Man, I can name a dozen that are smaller. Of the thousands of reptiles, maybe a dozen species, pythons, monitors, alligators, crocodiles, grow any larger than a hundred pounds. We are familiar with the giant dinosaurs, but most species were small, right down to the size of chickens. Skinny chickens. Of all of the flocks of birds, there is only the ostrich. And of the insects, in their historical hundreds of millions of species, not one, in all of the lifetime of the planet, has even approached the mass of a *Homo sapiens* child. We are giants, and most of us seek out other giants, creatures of comparable magnitude, as if the others, the vast majority, are beneath our notice. And that is exactly where most wildlife is: *Beneath* our notice. We look outward, and upward, and notice what is there. We do not look down. We should. Try it. You will see.

I am sitting in a cluster of wild rose. The blossoms are all gone, but the hips are not yet ripe. There are thick stands of tall yellow flowers, and a few purple thistles, all rising from a substrate of thick grass. A couple of feet away runs the Cimarron River, a young river, only ten feet wide and a foot deep, clean and cold, bouncing over rocks and swirling around stranded driftwood, waving long streamers of green algae. An island lies near the other side, fifteen feet long, four feet wide, and so thickly grown with grass and riparian weed that not a speck of sand or silt can be seen. The far bank is a dense mass of fingerling willow and a couple of cottonwoods, and again, no sign of soil between bank and brook. This is the setting. This is the scene. This is the theater where the wildlife will stage their play.

The Little Folk are prey. Even the predators among them are in constant danger from hawk and coyote and bobcat and lynx. They hide, ever alert for any threat. And anything bigger than them is considered a threat. Even the two-legs, disgusted, nauseated at just the thought of eating a mouse or a lizard, is feared, and his presence alone is enough to freeze the tiny creatures in terror. No, not just the presence; the two-legs must also move. If he is still for a long enough time, the prey will forget him, or at least decide he is not dangerous, and will move, warily, and go about their business.

The butterflies ignore me. They likely have no idea I am here. Perhaps they have no ideas in the first place. Wee white things, with wingspans less than two inches, they flutter and flit an utterly erratic flight, investigating, searching for I know not what, for they almost never light. They cross my sight from right to left, borne on the slight downstream breeze, and wander away to vanish in the distance. The occasional fly arrives, and oddly (for a fly) departs and does not return. A sweat bee comes and hovers motionless a few inches from my shirt, intrigued by the blue color,

so rare in the woods. Now that I have been here, unmoving, long enough to be nominated for the status of a normal fixture, the scanty swallows and petite finches return. The thick-set willows, though shorter than me, are twenty times the height of the birds, and provide welcome protective perches bearing succulent insects among the tangled twigs. These undersized predators are ever so happy to dine in such a fine waterfront bistro, which they rate five stems and a beak and a claw. With the return of the birds, the miniature mammals are emboldened, and begin to stir, one eye on the birds and some attention on the motionless mass that was a two-legs, at least when it was moving. A minute mouse courageously emerges from a rose bush two feet from my toes, and dashes across a wide clearing twenty times his size (that is, thirty inches). A wary chipmunk, or perhaps it is a ground squirrel, timorously peeks from the sheltering foliage by the island, peers at me for a moment, then sips from the stream before slipping back into concealment. A ten-inch trout seems to materialize among the algae fronds. How long has he been there? He dashes across five feet of rapid current into a higher pool, and vanishes into the deeper water. A sleek brown streak of fur leaps from behind the island and slips into the river, sliding swiftly downstream. So fast was the passage that I cannot be certain, but I do believe it was an otter. She startled the songbirds, in any event, for she moved, and suddenly, and was many times their size. It is a frighteningly dangerous world, this microcosmic environment, as that fly just found out, sucked down by the trout in the pool. A bed of algae is being slowly tattered by a pair of crayfish, either eating the algae, or consuming creatures within it. Another ground squirrel is drinking at the same spot as the earlier one. By chipmunk standards, this is probably the best watering spot for, oh, several hundreds of inches.

Then the birds flee aloft, and three or four voles reveal their presence by sudden motion and sudden absence. Three tiny two-legs, children, have come to play in the water. They are tiny to me, but Brobdingnagian to my Lilliputian friends. The trout dives deep, the crayfish scuttle into hiding under the algae mat, and the only movements remaining are the slight swaying of the plants in the gentle breeze, and the swift splashing of the crystal waters, foaming and flashing in the afternoon sunlight.   And one white butterfly, staggering through the air, and no doubt singing a silly little song of carefree abandon.

And, do you know, I did not see one percent of the Little Folk who live here.

Interlude in a Meadow

Somehow, I have done it again. I seem to gravitate to spots like this, all the same, and all different. Sitting in solid shade, surrounded by bright sun, clear sky and scattered clouds overhead, sweet pine-clad hills all around against a background of deep gray thunderheads in every direction. The clouds call to each other in rumbling grumbles, discussing the hills and deciding what to drench and what to merely intimidate, sometimes striking at seemingly random trees, flashing their thunderbolts for no apparant reason. Are they gardeners studying the forests, watering where needed, pruning, starting small fires to sweep up accumulations of dead branches? I do not know their reasoning. It is above me.

The spot I have happened upon is a small grassy lea next to, of course, a musical stream, and bordered by wild rose, long past blossoming, and tall yellow flowers just in their prime. Cottonwoods and willows provide cool dimness, and an impudent four-foot juniper struts from the very edge of the laughing water, wriggling its roots in fine bown silt and rich sticky black mud. Tiny frogs settle in the mud, and leap to catch tinier insects, belly-flopping into the stream, then crawling back to the bank a few feet downstream. It is a constant migration, the army of amphibians slowly making their way through an array of eddies and pools. Do they all swim back upstream at night, or are more recruits constantly hatching in the headwaters? Another frog leaps to seize an unfortunate fly, then falls to the water, and falls in turn to a feeding trout. The trout is lucky to be where it is. Not only is there a take-out buffet of fresh frogs delivering themselves in a steady stream, but the nearest fisherman is fifty yards away, on the other side of the island.

If it were not for the fisherman, I would not realize there is an island spread before me. It is a lush, grassy field, abounding in trees and bushes and weeds, just like the lea in which I sit, and the lands to either side, and behind me. Only the clue that the river at my feet flows west to east, and the fisherman stands off to the South, proves he is working a different channel. That and the fact that, now I notice, the stream here is only half as wide as I should expect.

Little birds flit above the island, swooping, diving, cutting didos in their erratic pursuit of insects invisible to me. A woodpecker lights on a tree beside me, then leaps to the other side, where short snags will surely harbor plentiful insects.

The reason I came here was that I had gone to town for a new notebook, and as long as I was there, might just as well get some ice cream. I stopped by at some friends' camp to see if they needed anything, and they thought ice cream was a great idea. When I returned, they were off doing whatever, so I sat to wait, and write. One of them came back a short while ago and settled down with her crochetting. We smiled greetings, but said not a word. The best friends are those with whom you can share a space and feel no need to chatter. We sat in silence till the other woman arrived, then we shared our treat and chatted a bit. Now one has gone for a nap, the other is lying in the stream, and I am continuing this episode. The shade has shifted, the fisherman is gone, but the tranquillity remains. The thunder still rumbles, and the clouds have closed in, erasing the blue, spreading shade everywhere. The froglings still leap, the trout still feeds, the waters still chatter as they leapfrog over submerged stones. And now the thunderheads, perceiving that the ice cream is finished, begin to edge closer, drifting in our direction. Soon, I expect, rain will begin to fall. If it becomes thick and strong, I shall retire to my tent, for I cannot write in the rain; the paper becomes too fragile. Until then, I shall stay here with friends, two-legged, four-legged, web-footed, finned and feathered.

There is nothing, in plain, hard fact, that is better to do.

The Goddess

The great sand deserts of the Middle East have spawned many religions, possibly more than any other land. There are those of Marduk and Ba'al, of Ishtar and Zoroaster, of many more gods long forgotten by all but archaeologists, and surely many forgotten completely. Some have survived and grown, and still impact the world most strongly; Judaism, Christianity, Islam. All born in the great open spaces that shout "Hey, dummy, there is more to the world than just rocks and trees!"

Religious experiences great and small are also produced by the mountains. I know of no religion born in a city except Confucianism, and that one is more of a bureaucratic manual. (Trust the Chinese to find bureaucracy spiritual.) Vast vistas of self-regulating stable eco-systems drive home the point: "Do you really think something this perfect and complete could happen by accident?" And once you are attuned to the spiritual world, you see it everywhere. It even influences your view of the mundane. Just as the materialist can view the spiritual and see only the material, so can the spiritualist see the material, and flavor it with the divine. This might be exactly what the Chinese did.

I did so today. I saw a goddess. She is Piscella, goddess of fish. She is the one to whom fishermen pray, begging the boon of quiet waters teeming with abundant fish, for hungry trout that will snap at their flies and provide a good fight, for a well-filled creel, and for a splendid beer-battered fish fry. And she answered their prayers, and did bless the waters with a profusion of fat trout, not two, but *three* full scoops of them.

It was a cloudy day, solid overcast dropping spates of rain off and on. In the midst of the gloom, a single ray of sunlight pierced the clouds and fell upon the road, illuminating a great white truck. The holy truck stopped beside the river, and She emerged from the cab. She did stand upon the great tank which was borne upon the back of the truck, and caused to open a mighty portal upon the top. Into the cistern did She dip a net, and lo, it emerged bearing a full cubic cubit of writhing and flopping fish! Thrice did She do thus, bearing Her benefice even unto the river, casting Her largesse upon the waters, and bidding them to go forth and multiply. Multiply the pleasures of the fishermen flocking to the banks.

It is a common sight in New Mexico and Arizona. Fishing is far too popular to by supported by the natural supply of fish, so it must be supplememented by the artificial. Yes, these fish are artificial. That does not mean the fish are imitation, or inferior to the naturally bred. It means they are spawned and raised by skilled arts. By artifice. Artificial. Just like a field of wheat sown and tended by man is artificial, even if it is organically grown. In fact, these fish are larger, healthier, fatter than their wild cousins, for they have been raised under controlled conditions, well fed, and protected from diseases and parasites and predators. The eggs are fertilized in flasks of flowing waters, and cherished till they hatch, and are spawned into huge tanks of clear, clean waters. They are fed regularly, and exercised by a constant current, until they are fully grown. Then they are harvested, loaded into tank trucks, and Piscella, in her many avatars, transports them to the Promised, uh, Waters. When the wandering is accomplished, they are taken up and enter into their Paradise. "Hosannah!" the fish cry. "We are here, we are in the Wild, we are free!" And there they joyfully scatter to the pools and the rapids, to the logs decaying in the waters, and they gobble the minnows and tadpoles and flies ... and hooks. And thus they fulfil their destiny, perched on poles, or bathed in batter and flipping on the skillet, frying to a beautiful brown, then placed upon a plate and consumed. With tartar sauce. Heavenly!

This is as things should be. There are so many people who find so much pleasure in the game of fishing. There is no sight more beautiful than a little girl landing her very first fish, no music more pleasing than her lilting laughter and spontaneous squeal of joy. But there are too many fishermen for our natural bounty to accommodate, and so we must take precautions. Some waters are closed to fishing. Others are restricted to catch-and-release.   Some are productive enough, and unfrequented enough, to take care of themselves. The rest are artificially stocked. Hatcheries and distribution systems, paid for by the sale of licenses, provide ample fish for the sportsmen. And the fish do not seem to mind. At least, I have never heard one to complain.

Perhaps I shall ask Piscella.

Palisades

A palisade is a wall to stop something, and to make something last longer. They are usually for protection, to keep an enemy out so the defenders will not die, sometimes for preservation, to hold back a hillside and keep it where it is a bit longer. They are commonly made of tree trunks, shorn of branches, driven vertically into the ground, side by side, to form an unbroken wall. You have seen them; the common Hollywood depiction of a cavalry fort is a palisade.

Rock walls sometimes take on the rough appearance of a palisade, and often are named "The Palisades". Of course, since there are so many, when you mention them to someone, you must specify which state they are in, or which part of the state. Bear's Tepee, which used to be called Devil's Tower, is the most famous and dramatic example of such stonework, but many states have there own versions. And many of them really do not look like palisades, but were named by muddy thinkers. And there are many, such as in Utah's Fremont Indian State Park, that could be called palisades, but are not.

I am sitting in the shade of great trees on the bank of the Cimarron River in New Mexico, within spitting distance of the water. The river is low now; if it was at full flood, my head would be underwater. Assuming I could sit still. Actually I would be tumbling down the river in pieces, for the river is steep here. There is a three-foot waterfall next to me, so loud that I cannot hear cars on the highway fifty yards away. That is one reason I have chosen this precise spot. Another is the surrounding trees, fifty and sixty foot pines and cottonwoods.

An arm's length away is one erect cottonwood corpse two feet in diameter. And all around me on the rocks and boulders fresh and sharp from their tumble down the cliffs, in the sand and silt still sodden from the heavy rains last night, lies the third reason, deep, cool shade, dappled a bit by the slanting rays of the sun that is just clearing the horizon. Since sunrise was more than three hours ago, you should realize the horizon is pretty far above me. And that is the fourth reason, the *real* reason I am sitting here.

The Cimarron River is gnawing slowly at the base of the Palisades, a formation of igneous rick called *sill* or *monzonite*, laid down forty million years ago, about the time this land grew bored with seaside (or seabed) living and decided to move to the mountains. Or move to *be* the mountains. They succeeded, and became the Rocky Mountains, and are still there, though the jealous waters still strive to bring them low again. They have done much, the waters have, clawing and grinding and gnawing away the rocks, till the ridges and plateaus stand a mere nine thousand feet above the level of the sea, perhaps half of what they had attained at their acme. And the waters have chewed deep canyons, such as the one I am in now, nibbling at the base of the cliff, a tactic more efficient than devouring from the top down, for by undermining a few feet of rock from the base, the waters can split off masses hundreds or thousands of feet high, shattering the mighty slabs into tiny fragments only ten or fifteen feet across. Such fragments are easily ground to dust in just a few fleeting centuries, which is an instant on the geological scale of time.

The sill has a crystalline structure, primarily vertical, which results in the falling rock leaving behind straight vertical cracks and seams in the remaining living bedrock, a pattern closely reminiscent of the vertical logs of a palisade, and thus the name. Monzonite is a pale rock, white and yellow and beige, almost red at its extreme. Much of the cliff is pale green or black, but those colors are not of the rock. As much as a fifth of the face is covered by lichen and fungus, mold that eats the rock itself. Such life grows very slowly, and this gives mute testimony to the vast (on our scale) amount of time required to crumble these cliffs. It is comforting, reassuring, for almost directly above me hangs an outcrop. Beginning about fifty feet below the top, the cliff leans steadily outward, till at the very lip, it projects at least ten feet from the vertical. If that mass should break and fall, it would plummet and shatter on the short sixty-degree talus bed, and ricochet as knife-edge shards and brutal bludgeons for two hundred feet in all directions, a blast from Gargantua's shotgun which I would surely not survive. Unless I ducked behind the cottonwood trunk beside me. But it is not going to happen, not now. The mountain will not fall on me. The ominous crag is about half covered by lichen. It has taken several decades at least for that layer to grow, so this potential hazard must have existed for at least that length of time. The odds against the threat being realized during the few hours I am here are geological.

But it does happen. Not far away I see a patch of cliff, sixty feet high, forty feet wide, right at the top. The color is fresher, redder, less pale, more sharp than the usual pastel, and unlike the rock immediately adjacent, it bears no lichen. None.

Directly below lies a small talus fan of much the same color, and protruding from it spring broken branches and a shattered stump. The branches still bear needles, though they are brown and red, not green at all. It is a tomb, a recent grave, and the gravedigger, the winter ice, has but recently departed. For this fall occured only a scant few months ago, and the top of the hundred-year-old tree still lies in the hands of the princely river. "Alas", it says, "Poor Ponderosa! I knew him, Lone."

In spite of the mounded talus and the piles of shattered stone, the ubiquitous boulders disrupting the freely flowing waters and making of them a wonderland of riffles and rapids, of short-lived but ever-present bubbles and foam, of chattering shallows and roaring waterfalls, despite the plethora of crumbled cliff-fragments,the palisades still stand tall, erect, unmoving. To see them from the road is to be captivated by their beauty. To view them from the river is to be stunned by their majesty.   To behold them from their base is to be paralyzed by their awesome mass, towering infinitely to the sky. It is said that familiarity breeds contempt, but the closer and more familiar you become to the Palisades, the more incredible and intimidating they become. They cannot be adequately described; no photographs can do them justice. When you visit them, be prepared to cross the river; it is rarely very deep, and while it is often dangerously swift, there are calm and gentle, fairly gentle, places where one can ford. Only when standing at their base, only when you are close enough to touch the wall, only then can you truly appreciate their glorious magnificence.   Do not deprive yourself of the experience. Please do not!

The Palisades are old as we view time, but young by the reckonings of rocks. Born in magmatic fire and thrust into the sky, for long multitudes of millenia they lay buried. Only recently were they exposed to the air, and now they are peeled away, layer by layer, by the unrelenting water. The rock is riven and broken and crushed, forced to be its own millstones, grinding itself to dust and earth, sill converted to silt, and borne a thousand miles to extend the Mississippi Delta, excreted into the Gulf of Mexico. And there it will lie for an age or two awaiting the arrival of the rest of the clan, till the Palisades are gone, powdered like the wood of a prehistoric palisade. There they will reside till the continent rolls in its restless sleep, and the seabed we know becomes a new range of mountains half a billion years from now.

But now they are still here, grand, majestic, beautiful. You should take the time, make the chance to come see them. They will not be here forever.

Requiem

I was not sure if I should include this chapter, for this book is largely intended to share special sites, to encourage others to visit them. I had wonderful times at Cimarron Canyon. I made happy memories. I met gold friends. I will always treasure it, and would share it with as many people as possible.

But it is no longer there.

The forest was overburdened with flammables, pine needles and dead leaves, fallen branches and snags, failed saplings and withered bushes, the refuse of a century of suppressing every natural fire. The Winter had been terribly arid; no snow had fallen at all. The weather was hot, dry, and above all, windy. The fire danger was beyond Extreme; it could not possibly have been worse.

Wildfire swept the canyon this year. I can hope the reports are exaggerated; the road is closed, so I cannot see for myself. But the trees, I am told, are gone. The Palisades are stained with smoke, the cool shaded spot from which I admired them bakes in the sun. The meadow of the Interlude is black and bare. Blackjack no longer offers any reason to pack your gear in; you might just as well camp in the parking lot of Ponderosa. Tolby is lifeless; site 2 is moist ashes on the riverbank. The hardy and tough cottonwoods, survivors of hundreds of years of travail, will no longer fall before the twisting winds, for Fire conquered them first. The Little Folk have gone away, those that survived. The Goddess no longer stocks the stream, for there are no fishers to benefit. Only the moonlight and starlight are left to bathe the rocks.

In the end, I chose to keep this chapter, as a memorial. The Canyon itself still remains, and the river continues its campaign against the cliffs. Nature does heal herself; the forest will recover, as it has done so many, many times before. The area will be enjoyable again in a decade or two, but it will require centuries to fully restore itself, for the great pines and cottonwoods grow slowly. Until then, perhaps people will read these tales, these ghosts of what once was, then ride through the canyon and see what our foolishness has done. Perhaps they will be a bit more cautious with fire. Perhaps another paradise will be spared this doom.

I am afraid I have to end off now. The paper has become too soggy.

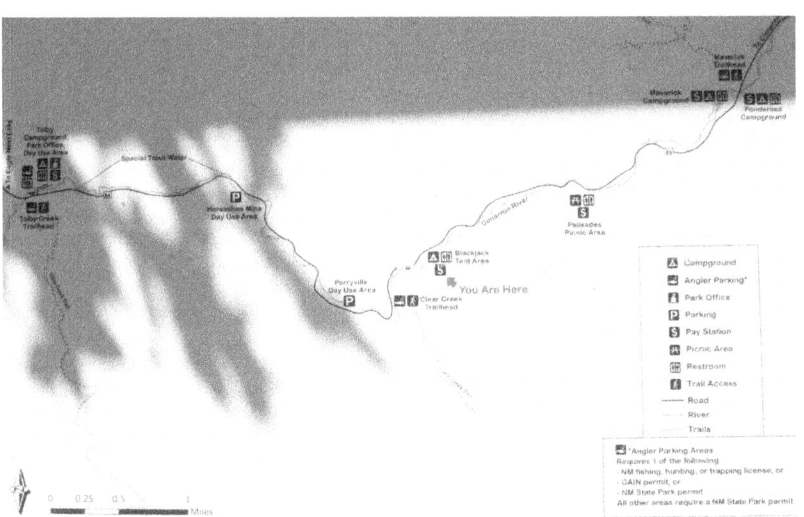

**Welcome to
Cimarron Canyon
New Mexico State Park**

Sugarite Canyon

New Mexico

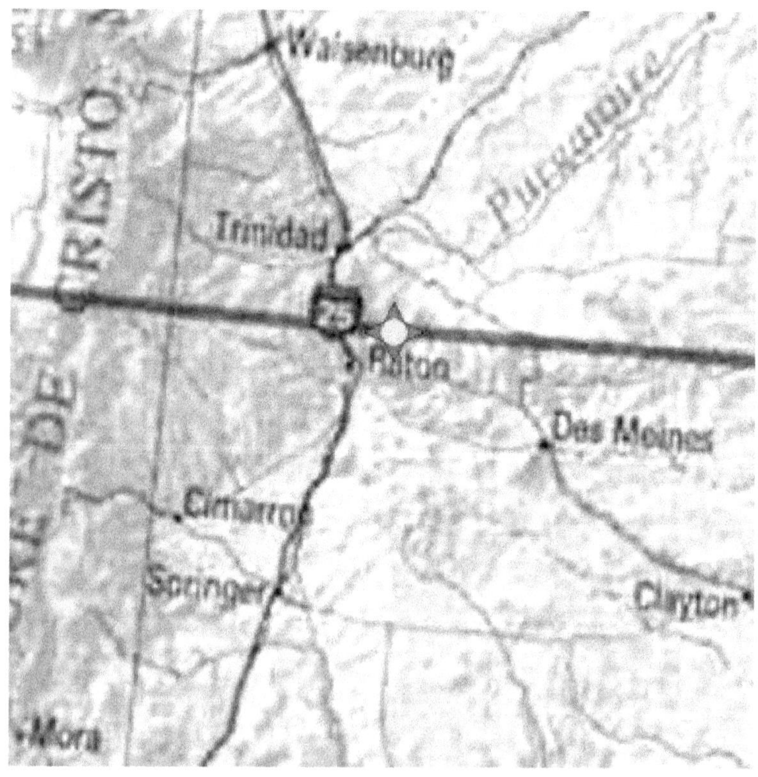

Sugarite Canyon

Each of the New Mexico State Parks is unique in some way (or in several ways), but they all share one particular characteristic: They are (relatively) dry.   Not too surprising, since New Mexico is, basically, a dry state. It has rivers, but Easterners would think them brooks, and lakes, on the scale of New England ponds. Aside from about two months each year (usually), rain is a rare event. This does not mean the land is barren; the native flora is perfectly well adapted. There are not only trees, there are forests. There are some areas of sandy "waste", home of mesquite, cactus and the gila monster, but there is even more solid grassland. Brush and wildflowers and, almost everywhere, cactus. Sometimes they are sparse, each plant several feet from the next, but they are there, with their associated fauna, as sparse or abundant as the local plants.

Not Sugarite Canyon. If you took photographs of each of the New Mexico parks and mixed them in with pictures of parks in other states, you could pick out the parks in New Mexico (along with Arizona and West Texas), but you would miss Sugarite Canyon. It just does not *look* like the others.
The rocks are much the same, broken boulders jutting from the soil, striated scars of bedrock seaming the sides of the steep canyon walls. But where the other parks are dominated by Ponderosa Pine and Juniper, here many, perhaps most, of the trees are Rocky Mountain White Oak, Gambel Oak. Bushes of chokecherry are abundant. The ground among the trees is not mostly bare, but is completely covered by lush growth such as burdock and many grasses.

Why? Why is this place so different, so lush, so alive? Water. There are many springs in the area, which feed the Chicorica Creek and its tributaries, and three dams along the creek to provide reservoirs that are always full. And there is nothing upstream to use the water, nothing but the native ecosystem. No ranches or farms or villages. The waters flow from the Lake Dorothey State Wildlife Area in Colorado. All the way from Colorado, almost three miles north of here. Thus, though it rarely rains here, the air is often humid. Dew is not uncommon. Bare dirt, where there is any, looks as dry and arid as the stereotype of New Mexico would imply, but an inch down or less, the soil becomes moist.

Being about a mile and a half up, the area is cooler. With all of the vegetation, a lot of moisture is transpired, evaporated from the leaves, which further cools the air. There is no treeless patch as large as an acre, so there is ample shade. The

Alice Lake Campground is the most comfortable in any New Mexico State Park, except possibly Morphy Lake. (Cimarron Canyon used to be able to compete, but alas, it was recently swept by wildfire. This area was also burned off a few years ago, and bears superb testimony to the forest's ability to regenerate and recover.) Given all of this in its favor, it is odd that Sugarite Canyon is not better known. Those who do know it, love it and return year after year. Alice Lake Campground has sixteen sites, twelve with water and electricity. Eleven sites are reservable. Soda Pocket Campground, several hundred feet higher, has twenty four sites, no reservations, no electricity, no water at campsites (there is one water spigot, non-functional when I was there), but it does have vault toilets, and magnificent views. It is reached via over a mile of dirt road, well-maintained, but with some washboarding and shallow gullies, and several steep slopes. Still, it is well worth traversing, because beside the views, the best trails start from Soda Pocket.

There are more birds, and more species of birds, ranging from hummingbirds to wild turkeys, because the undergrowth sports such a quantity and variety of seeds and insects. You will likely spot a sugarite (pronounced shu-gah-REET), which is not a mineral, but the Indian name for a local bird. Mule deer are ubiquitous; I have never done the mile-and-a-half ride from my campsite to the showers without seeing at least one deer, and once an elk. Black bears are plentiful, and mountain lions, while not plentiful, are not rare. There are many foxes and coyotes, but you will rarely see them. I have seen beaver dams in the park, though not the beaver themselves. On the way in to the park, I saw a herd of pronghorn, and another of bison. Not a bison ranch, but a wild herd. Prairie chickens, prairie dogs, red squirrels, ground squirrels, chipmunks, all of the wildlife associated with the Old West is still here.

If you have no reservation, you will almost certainly find an open campsite if you arrive in the middle of the week. I still recommend reserving, but do *not* choose Alice Lake site 4. It is terrible, so bad that I always try to get it, so that others will not have to suffer.

What the Hey?

Now, look: Sugarite Canyon is relatively unknown. Why? I have no idea. It is beautiful, the climate is comfortable, there are several lakes with good fishing, beautiful trails both easy and difficult, plentiful birds for watching, all sorts of wildlife, from chipmunks to bison, here and nearby, there is a town with stores (including R&D Honda, an excellent bike service shop) only seven miles away, and the park even has free hot showers! But it is not that heavily used. It is quite rare, almost unheard of, for every campsite to be occupied. This is very unusual.

The park is lush, especially by New Mexico standards. *Lots* of plants, full ground cover of grasses and weeds and wildflowers. The trees are mostly oak and locust instead of pine and juniper. There are three lakes, reservoirs, actually, and all three are brim full, even during drought. No waterlines ten feet above the surface, not here. Also very unusual.

The place used to be a coal mine. Yes, there is coal in New Mexico, and oil, too. It is long abandoned, pretty much nothing left but the mineshafts, a few bits of machinery, the cemetary and post office (which is restored as the Visitor Center). There are several hiking trails among the mine area, but the trails, as trails, are far more interesting than the stated reason for them. Undoubtedly, unusual.

But this is too much. All experienced campers and RVers know you do not arrive at a campground on Saturday, certainly not if you have no reservation. Tuesday, Wednesday, Thursday, those are good days; you will almost always find a vacant site in the middle of the week. And once you are settled in, you do not *leave* on a Saturday. Okay, maybe if you are on a two week trip and it will take two days to get home. Not otherwise.

This is Saturday. Fourteen out of the sixteen sites are occupied. Two of the occupants are overnighters. Two are hosts. Eight of the remaining ten leave. I know that at least four of them live less than a day's travel away. This makes no sense. After all of the trouble and expense to get here, why not enjoy an additional day? Maybe one of them works on Sunday, but surely not all eight. Ten of them, really, for two of the sites were occupied by double parties, pairs from different states rendezvousing here for a shared vacation. That happens a lot.

But it became even stranger. One after another, those vacated sites were reoccupied, even the four that were not by reservation. Four of the new-comers arrived on a Saturday with no reservations. Inexperience? Chutzpah? Or maybe they are familiar with the park and *knew* they had a good chance of getting a likely site?

No. No, I think it is pretty much random. On Monday morning every site was full, including all seven overflow sites. Wednesday saw two vacant sites, and four of the overflow. What campground is most full on weekdays? (Outside of a National Park.)

It is most unusual. But since the park itself is so unusual, I guess it is normal.

Music in Motion

The sky is mostly overcast. Great clouds in a thick web of open blue dash across the sky, for they are low, and the land is high, and the wind is very strong. Since this is a canyon, and it twists and winds between the cliffs, the speed and intensity of wind at ground level varies, from corpselike calm to frenetic gust. Loose papers lift and leap among the flowers, dust swirls among the stones, and city girls clutch their hair in gasping despair. Fishers curse as their boats cluster onto the lee shore, and hikers gasp in alarm and stagger away from cliff rims. The timid and the unimaginative huddle inside their rigs, where the frivolous flurries will not water their eyes nor rustle their books. I sit in the semi-shade and watch the trees.

Trees take a holiday when the wind frolics among them. Their reasons are identical: They move with the wind. Their actions, their styles, are as varied as their leaves. Forests of towering ponderosas sway in stately semi-unison, lifting their hands in solemn praise of something larger than themselves. Stands of spruce and fir bob and twist in waves compliant to the currents of air. Groves of oaks stand firm, outer leaves fluttering frantically, twigs nervously twitching, lesser limbs nodding and bowing, boughs barely moving, and boles not deigning to submit to any motion at all. Arrays of aspen frenziedly flutter their two-tone leaves, twisting and dancing and celebrating the chance to move. Each plays its own melody, each dances to its own tune.

This forest is symphonic. Most of the elders are Gambel Oaks, dominating the lesser and lighter locusts. Now and then a pair of Ponderosa Pines looms above the general level, and here beside me two majestic White Firs split the difference between oak and pine. A rolling carpet of grass and weed and wildflower thickly cloaks the thin soil, save where the slopes are too steep, and stones are exposed amid dirt and dead leaves. And between the carpet and the crowns springs the body of the greenery, a swelling orchestration of seedlings and saplings, from six inches to sixteen feet, oaks and locusts of every shape and size, densely crowded on the one hand, thinly scattered on the other.

And it is all in motion, no, in *motions*. Each gust brings an agitation, a surge and swell, as all of the leaves bow in unison. Then the trees respond, first the smallest, then the larger, each tree reacting more slowly as its relative size increases. They recoil together, again the smallest returning soonest. A second gust in the midst of this recoil randomizes the motion, and for a moment it seems as if every tree is being blown by a different wind. If the gust should continue as a steady wind, the little trees will bend away, nodding and straightening, but never swaying back past the vertical. The entire forest is in motion, and it is easy to suspect the trees are the source, that they are reaching, straining, even walking. At first glance, at only a superficial look, it all appears chaotic, unplanned, uncontrolled, unrelated.   Each tree, each branch, each leaf, moves independently of all others, and yet with them, in the most complex close harmony ever conceived. Locusts vibrate in a fandango like the staccato of a Spanish dancer's heels. On smaller oak saplings, the leaves twist, and on larger ones they polka. Their trunks reel and jig, the massive elders turn in a minuet, their twig-tips barely touching, and the ground grasses bounce and sway like the little children enraptured by the square-dance antics of their elders. The rhythm and tempo are called by the wind, as energetic and ecstatic as a First Negro Baptist Sunday Service, or as stately and solemn as a formal Catholic Mass, and between these extremes, in every variation, the landscape dances before the Lord with all its might. The thunderous crescendo of a gust-front sweeps the groves in accompaniment with a flowing roll of thunder, and the dancers rest in a brief intermission, taking refreshment in light rain. A fanfare of bright sunbeams announces the Second Movement, and the ball begins anew.

Each gust is a song of its own. Each hour is an opus, each day is a concert. The wind in the forest is music for the eyes. Enjoy it when you can, for each concert is unique, a jam session by a full orchestra; it will never be repeated, never. But if you should miss one, do not be distraught: There will always be another, and just as good.

Vedauwoo

Wyoming

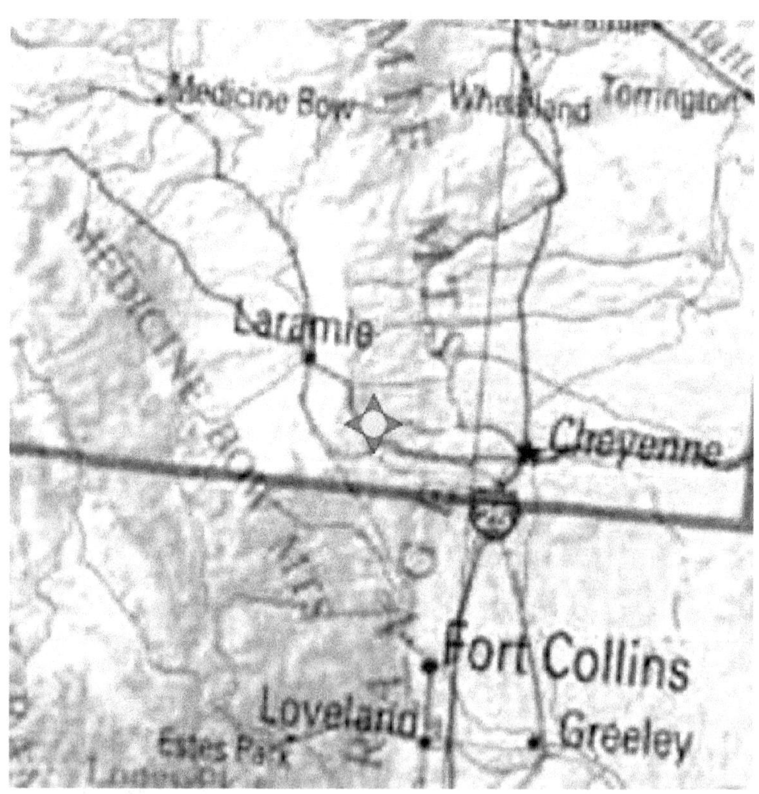

Vedauwoo

Vedauwoo is a campground in the Medicine Bow National Forest. Many of the campgrounds in that Forest do not provide drinking water, and those that do, often do not. At least, in every one in which I have stayed, the water system was shut down. Fortunately, Vedauwoo is only six miles from a forest Visitor Center, where one can fill up water bottles and tanks. There is a fairly heavily travelled highway a half mile south, visible, with no forest or ridges between to block or muffle the sound. However, it is not loud, and not an annoyance.

Aside from that, the campground is nearly perfect. Little wildlife is visible, just a few birds and squirrels and a multitude of tiny chipmunks, the second smallest I have ever seen. There are not a lot of trees. Just enough. It is the rocks that are almost unbelievable, plentiful and beautiful massive boulders that are not boulders, having never been in any stream or river, but carved into fantastic sculptures nonetheless. But the trees and the rocks (and the weather) merit essays of their own. Here I am writing of the campground itself.

There are two sections. One has twenty four sites, some of which can take a fairly large motor home or trailer, but none suitable for anything longer than about forty feet or so. The other is labelled "tents only". You can drive in, but no trailers or RVs are allowed. When I was there, this tent section was completely empty. That is not surprising, because there is a sign that says "Camping", with the little tent symbol, pointing to the main campground, but no such sign for the tents-only section. There is even a sign on the road to it, "No campers or trailers beyond this point". You have to know it is there.

Firewood gathering is allowed, but there is little available Not in the campgrounds. However, there are several trails and day-use areas, Beaver Cliff, Box Canyon, The Gazebo, and there is plenty of dead-and-down wood among them, for these back areas are heavily wooded right up to the cliffs from which the campground takes its name.   Thick stands of aspen predominate, but large pine trees, some of them giants, and junipers are common. There are many picnic sites with tables and fire rings scattered about, but no overnight camping. Some are sited under great overhanging rocks, not jutting bedrock, but worn stones thirty feet through, some seeming to be delicately balanced.

There are a couple of paved trails, wide and smooth, easily traversed by wheelchairs. The others are dirt, and mostly pretty easy walks. Besides a stroll among cool trees, the trails offer spectacular views of the granite cliffs, renowned among rock-climbers for some of the finest crevices, or so I am told. I am not a rock-climber, but if you are, you will love this place!

I first came here unintentionally for an overnight stop, and did not leave for five days. I expect you will love it as I do. It is the best campground I know of for many miles.

Falling In Love Again

Every place is magical, some more than others. Even cities have magic, each of its own unique flavor. Hollywood, for example, is steeped in the True Madness, as great actors have described their art, the magic of the stage, a contagious, self-propagating magic. New York City, where Broadway is imbued with some of the same magic as Hollywood, and where Wall Street transforms paper into profit, and millions of people are trapped in the webs of the wizardry. Washington, D.C., from where skilled sorcerers cast spells upon the entire nation, even the whole world, transforming reality to fit their desires. The magic of the Wild Places is different, for in the cities, it is Human Magic that is dominant, created by humans for human purposes, and affecting the Wilds only indirectly, if at all. In the Wilds there is Wild Magic, often created by the wilderness denizens for their own purposes, but also created by the land itself for reasons incomprehensible, sometimes imperceptible to a two-legs, but still there. We can see the results, and we usually ascribe them to chance and coincidence. But whether we are aware of it or not, whether we are willing to admit it or not, we are affected by the wild spells and cantrips. We feel them. Unbeknownst to us, our actions and ideas alter under their influence. But if our awareness is great enough, if we are open to new and different ideas, if we are willing to be proven wrong, to concede that maybe reality is not quite what we had believed it, had *known* it to be, then can we at least begin to perceive and understand the Wild Magic. And then we can embrace it, and become enhanced by it, become more than we were before. And a new world, the *real* world, opens before our senses, and our minds.

I came to Vedauwoo quite by accident. I was traveling north, from New Mexico to Bear's Tepee by the shortest and fastest route available (or so I thought). But Denver traffic took me by surprise. Midafternoon freeway traffic on a Wednesday should be fairly light, yes? No. In Los Angeles, it would be, but in Denver, it was worthy of a Los Angeles rush hour. (Rush hour: The time the traffic moves most slowly.) I reached Wyoming very late, and the Medicine Bow National Forest was drenched in rain, heavy and growing heavier. I had intended to stop at Tie City or Yellow Pine, but eight miles short of them lay Vedauwoo. It would get me off of the freeway and out of the rain that much sooner (nearly half an hour at the speed I could maintain), and I had never been there before. Three good reasons to visit. The rain stopped as I pulled in, and held off just long enough to get my tent pitched and gear stowed. Then it resumed. Immediately. Chance. Coincidence. Or the spells of some wise and benificent spirit steering me, herding me, as the hobbits were steered to the Withywindle by spells that made the path to the river easy, and all other paths impossible. (Of *course* this is fantasy! Do you really think I believe this to be hard scientific fact? All the same, it did happen.)

The night was cold and wet. I was warm and dry, and lulled by the soft sounds of rain and distant thunder. And the morning dawned clear and bright. Clouds swept across half of the sky, the setting moon visible over the western horizon. It was mid-summer, so the night had been short, and I was, as usual, the first to arise and welcome the new day. I wandered the campground, camera, as always, slung from my neck. I was amazed by the sights spread before me. Trees everywhere, but only singletons, pairs, small groves and copses, never enough to call a forest. Little grass, but a solid groundcover of bracken and weed and wildflower. The air was brisk, cool but not truly cold, and humid, heavy with unfallen dew. And rocks! Rocks of every size, from tadpoles to whales, and of nearly every shape imaginable, and more shapes that lay on the far side of imagination. And the sun rose among long and narrow clouds, bearing a magnificent pallet of fiery colors, silhouetting the stark skeleton of a perfect tree. I gathered

some of the best photographs I have ever seen. I was entranced, thoroughly entrapped by the spells of the land, of trees and flora and atmosphere and standing stones. The raindrops and dewdrops evaporated in the lucid light, and my plans evaporated with them. I had come for only a single night but now I would stay, and only the land knew how long.

I had fallen in love again. There are places that do that to me. Castle Rock, where the Goblin King reigns. Villanueva, which inspired sixteen stories in twelve days, and gave me a thousand pictures, worth a million words. Owen Creek, home of the perfect campsite. And now Vedauwoo, one of the oldest places on Earth, a center of beauty and magic of an intensity and concentration and variety such as I have never before experienced, where every third step treads on a new spell, a land mine, a booby trap which shatters and scatters sharp shrapnel, shards of magic that pierce the mind, causing it to bleed imagination that spatters the rocks and trees and paints on them images invoking thoughts and visions so profusely, even I cannot write them all down. But the unwritten ones are not lost, for the spells reset themselves, ready for the next stepper, wary or unwary, to set them off and spew their magic anew. No bare soul is immune to them, only the guarded ones, armored in counter-spells of disbelief and practicality, safely ensconced within walls of orthodoxy, behind doors of denial, barred with beams of unbreakable certainty, in mental bastions of insistence on the immutability of Physical Science, of iron faith in the infallibility of the scientists, the prophets of Truth. Those poor souls believe only what they are told to believe, that all Natural Law is known, that there is no possibility that their dogma is in any way wrong, or even slightly incomplete. They know, and therefor cannot learn. Pity them, for only those open to new ideas, only those with the courage to admit to being wrong, only those can learn new truths, can see new beauty, can realize that hard-held beliefs are no less fantasy than the visions released by a stepped-on spell.

And that is nowhere more true than here, in Vedauwoo. I rode into a fairy circle, and may never emerge, not entirely. But there is one absolute certainty: I will never, ever, forget.

The Bones of Vedauwoo

Vedauwoo (VEE-dah-voo) is an old Arapahoe word meaning "Earth". Not soil, or dirt, but the land, the planet, the body of the world. It is also the name given a rock formation in the Medicine Bow National Forest, so named because the rock is among the oldest in the world. When the young planet was still molten, and first cooled enough to begin to become solid, this rock, this granite, that which is now this cliff and ridge, was one of the bodies that hardened before any of the others.

A campground was established among the cliffs, and was given its name, and that was very appropriate, for while the visible cliffs stand tallest, still there are many ridges, long protrusions of the bedrock, breaking through the soil and ground broken from the Earth in the few million years since this part of the world was thrust upwards by the slow titanic collision of massive crustal plates. Erosion has carried away the younger rocks (and what a Herculean labor that must have been!) and left only a thin layer of recently broken sharp gravel and scattered stones, massive to us, but only miniscule splinters of the ancient bedrock, the oldest of the bones of Vedauwoo, the Earth.

The rocks look like boulders, weathered and round, but they are not. Boulders are rocks that have been rolled within rivers, ground and shaped and polished by sand and gravel impelled by the rushing waters. These rocks have not moved, except as gravity has made them fall when ice-filled crevices made them crack and split from their more-than-ancient places. These rocks have not been shaped save by ice from absorbed water and by the acids of lichens spreading on the surfaces, dulling sharp edges. So slow are the patient processes that the sand and gravel thus produced does not cling to the bases of the rocks like the talus that trims a mesa, but has been spread in a wide, flat plain by the battering of rain and the impetus of the wind. Like the bedrock itself, the fragmented rocks, and even the powdered soil are old, old.

And over time, the myriad of rocks have taken on shapes weird and eldritch, awaiting only an imagination active enough to bring them to life, to imbue thems with meaning, to waken suspicions of a cadre of sly and subtle sculptors working in stealth and secret, and quietly creating their gallery of art to rival and surpass the City of Rocks, and even the Louvre.

I came here for an overnight stop, a waystation from Here to There. But now I will not see Bear's Tepee this year, or check on Crazy Horse's progress, nor drop in on the Sturgis Rally. I will be lucky to get away in a week, for I have been entralled, ensorceled, bewitched. Just like at the Smithsonian Institute, a day is of no use. It takes at least a week to even begin to absorb the wonders abounding in this gallery.

Here is a face to rival New Hampshire's late Old Man of the Mountain. Here is a fortress as forbidding as Castle Rock. There is a mansion, a red White House, with a central portico and East and West Wings. A giant's wall looms, exactly like a New England stone wall, but each carefully placed stone is fifty feet across. A blockhouse standing sentinal on a distant ridge turns out to be a pair of rocks carved into near-perfect cubes, and separated from the bedrock below. Another face profiles from the mountain, and everywhere are grinning goblins thrusting their heads, buried to the chin, from their native soil. Walls of squared stone in level tiers divide the land. A fat-brained skull rests upon hard-bodied shoulders.

A cliff seamed by an abstract sculpture must submit to the indignity of two-legs insects crawling across its face. A bust caricatures Donald Trump in Thomas Jefferson's formal coat. A giant salamander or monstrous amphibian crawls from the Precambrian granite. A humpback whale cruises the soil, visible from blowhole to hump to tail. A tree-stump nestles against a monumental sculpture of itself, a stump of stone, complete to the bracing knees of roots embedded in the bedrock. A thin-snouted horse with a huge forehead surveys the land. A work in progress, a boulder being carved loose, stands on a narrow pedestal,

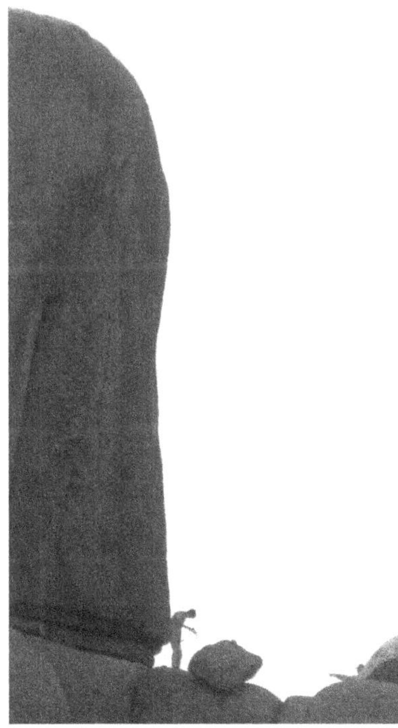

needing just a few more millenia before being completed. A hunch-backed dinosaur fumbles about, browsing on bushes that evolved millions of years after its own extinction. The original sphinx poses her riddle, "How did I come to be?" An elephant crushes its way through the trees. Stone toadstools sprout from the ground. A groundhog, a rockchuck, crouches on the duff. A stone giant lies prone, half buried, his shoulderblades and buttocks mooning the sky. Random rocks resemble nothing, but force you to ask, "How did *this* shape ever occur?"

This catalog is far from complete. It is like an hour at the Smithsonian. It is a glance in the front door of the Library of Congress. It is a one-page dictionary. There are many, many, *many* more rocks. And they change. They are different at dawn, at noon, at dusk. They change in the rain, and when the clouds descend to Earth. And most of all, most magically, most enchantingly, they change by the light of the full moon.

I have only spoken of the rocks. I have said nothing of the trees or the flowers. I have not touched upon the stars, which you can touch from here. Almost. Visit Vedauwoo. It is only sixteen miles east of Laramie. You can't miss it. Not till you have been there, and gone away. A day is not enough. A week is not enough. A single visit, unless you are very lucky, and the weather co-operates, is not enough. But do not worry. You have time. The bones of Vedauwoo are the bones of the Earth. They will be there for a while longer.

In a Cloud

People have a phrase "Wandering in a cloud'" It is a bad thing. It means thoughts are gray, unclear, misty . . . cloudy. It means one is not aware of the surroundings. There is nothing good about it, nothing to make it at all desireable.

I am wandering in a cloud right now. In the high hills, at eighty-six hundred feet. The day has been rainy, with a couple of thunderstorms, but now there is nothing. No sky, no rain, no clouds. Except one. One cloud has strayed a bit low, and I and the hills are caught up in it, enveloped by it, for all I know carried along with it. Visibility is less than two hundred feet, and there is no sound. Nothing. There is a highway, or used to be, about half a mile from my campsite. Big rigs, semis, were frequent, visible all day, audible, though barely so, all night. Not now. No motors groan in the distance. Thunder grumbles at long distance, but even that is brief. It does not echo as is its wont, especially here, where I once heard the claps echo and re-echo nonstop for sixteen minutes. The sound is dim and vague, gray, unclear, misty . . . cloudy.

The cloud is not like fog, not quite. It is reminiscent of fog, but there is a difference, obvious to the experienced, yet still very hard to describe. Fog tends to rise from the ground, and thins as it rises, till the sun dissipates it from the top down. Perhaps that is it, for a cloud grows denser as it gains altitude. It also spits a raindrop now and then, or a short-lived sprinkle. Fogs do not do that, they only condense, only leave a heavy dew. Whatever the difference may be, it is there, and I sense it, recognize it. I can always distinguish fog from a cloud.

A stand of trees caught my eye earlier today, a mix of living green and dead gray, sharply outlined against the blue and white sky. Now they are all black, the nearer ones perhaps hinting at the possibility of a touch of green, and stand in a uniform background of not-quite-white, not so much outlined against it as emerging from it. Another grove once held a uniformity of appearance in the crystalline air, and one could only tell which trees were closer, especially in the flatness of a photograph, by noting which nearer branches lay in front of the farther trees. Now it is clear, the perspective pierces the eye as each receding rank appears dimmer, less focused, as in a classic Japanese mountain painting. A rock, an extra-terrestrial skull, blood-raw from recent flaying, stood sharp and clear. Now it is dim, weathered, just an old bone. The cloudy mists have aged everything, leached away all of the bright bloom of youth, and draped all with the shroud of years. This morning the happy laughter of young children riding bicycles around the loop pierced the golden air; now they are gone, perhaps huddled indoors, insulated from the world and reality by walls and television. But the world remains, silent, and reality is vague.

Between the trees I see a dim grayness, but it is not the uniform cloud-color of the sky. There are shapes in it. Judging by their appearance, they could be snow on an alp, or a cliff of broken rocks, or a group of clouds, an incipient thunderhead. Reality has changed. It is not the same as it was a few hours ago. The sky is not a mass of clouds, distinct, individual, competing with a blue that would prefer to be ubiquitous. Now it is featureless, or rather, has but one feature, the uniform and unvaried gray. This morning there was a horizon, with awesome arrays of ancient rocks. Now there is no horizon at all. The foreground fades in the middle distance, and somewhere beyond blends into the sky. There is no point at which the sky clearly begins, for beyond fifty feet, nothing is clear. At my feet, the shapes and colors of flowers are sharp and tightly focused. In the near distance they are neither. They fade, and blur, and vanish. A tree that, close at hand, was precise in every detail, now, fifty yards later, is still a tree, but nothing else, not even its height, is definite. As most people's memories fade with time, so do present objects fade with distance. The cloud has taken on aspects of time. Instead of droplets of moisture, it comprises condensations of seconds and minutes. It has sucked time from the world, so that here, where I stand, there is no time. I can stay here forever, if I so choose.

I am wandering in a cloud. My thoughts are bright, clear, sharp. And I am alone. All of the other campers are huddled behind their walls doing something or other. I want to call them out, but they would not come. The outdoors is dreary, dull, uninteresting, they are sure of it, and have no interest in looking. All of them. Except one.

She materializes from the mist, stalking through the moist dimness, as I do, taking it in, absorbing whatever it holds and means to her. We greet, and agree the world is beautiful. She comments that she is composing a poem. Ah! I must not interrupt. If you finish soon, I would like to hear it. I am in that canvas tent.

We part, and fade in each other's distance.

Perhaps she shall title it "In a Cloud".

Wyoming Thunder

It started just a bit after noon, some twelve miles east of Laramie. Dawn had been silent, cloudless and cool, but not chilly. As the sun rose higher, an occasional cloud wandered past, white, shiny and innocent. Later, a few more, and a few more. By midday they filled the sky, and some dangled streaks of rain.

A single hailstone fell right in front of me. I checked the camp to be sure that nothing which rain could harm had been left out. A few drops fell, here, there, and off in the distance. Slowly, steadily, the number increased, joined by infrequent rumbles. I decided the clouds weren't fooling around, and moved into the tent.

I like to hear the patter of rain on the fly, a soft, not-quite-sharp tapping, especially when it is only two or three drops per second. There is no pattern or rhythm, not even what could be called a syncopation, not quite. Always, it almost seems as if there is a pattern that you are on the verge of perceiving, just like the words which you can almost make out in a swift and stony stream. But it never fulfils the promise.

The almost-rhythm grew faster and faster till the excited taps merged into a continuous static. As the last bit of blue hid behind the clouds I realized the distant thunder had become continuous, and had continued without a break for at least a minute. I noted the time. The rumble continued. There were no sharp cracks, just echoes as the sound danced among the hills that stretch for miles in all directions. It would peal loudly in the west, then diminish, passing to the south and fading in the east, and vanishing under another burst before it could fade completely away.   Several voices would enter in stately succession, maintaining a loud argument for a minute or more before slipping toward silence. Sometimes it would be reduced to a quiet "bum-bum-bum" promising to die at last, but always a fresh tongue brought new vigor to the debate. Ever the sullen roar would fade and fade, and I would listen and listen, hoping for and fearing the return of silence, and ever the thunder would renew and restore the endless rumble. Fade and freshen, fade and freshen, over and over and over, rumbling and tumbling as each hill spoke its piece. The speech continued, rose and fell, faded and ...

Silence.

After sixteen minutes and twenty seconds.

Silence.

For less than four seconds before the rebuttal began. They lasted more than two hours, these speeches of the lightnings and the commentaries of the hills. I timed no more, but each oration lasted several minutes, and no pause was more than a few seconds. The counterpoint by the rain was always there, stronger and weaker, faster and slower. The voices faded, till silence was longer than speech. The patter faded to taps, to nothing. Blue pushed clouds aside.

Silence.

Owen Creek

Wyoming

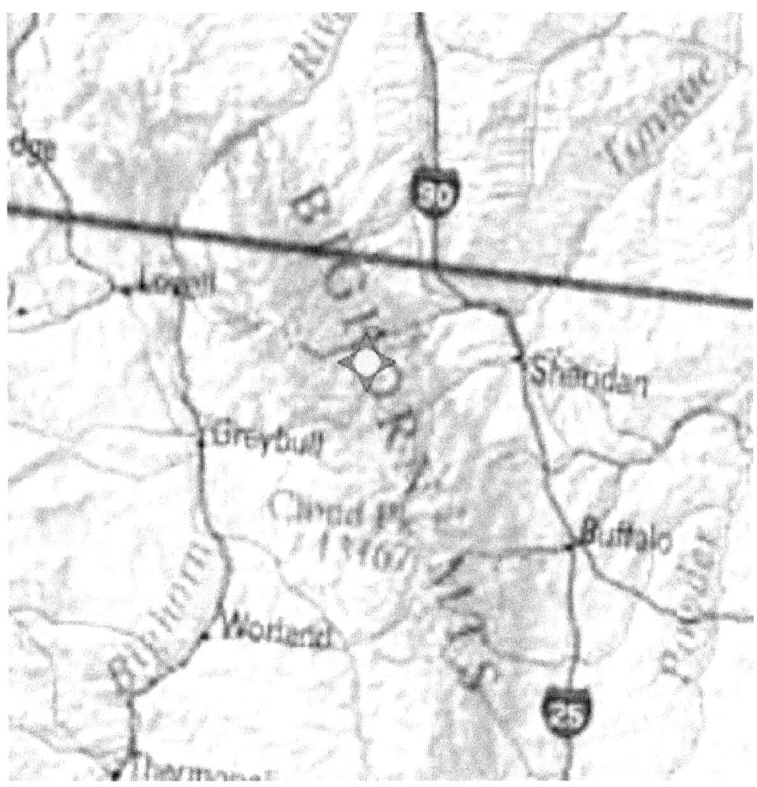

Perfection

The Perfect Stream lies high in the mountains, a mile and a half above the level of the sea. It is wide, ten to fifteen feet, with deep pools on either side of the swift current, pools where dwell native trout, not stocked. Several large boulders break the flow and force the current left and right, creating rapids and riffles and standing waves, whirling eddies and short-lived foam. The far bank is soft silt, buried beneath masses of lush grass and water-loving plants, leaves trailing in the water, providing shade and shelter to minnows and tadpoles. Many flowers of red and yellow, purple and white enhance the dozens of shades of green. Crowds of young cottonwood compete with aggressive lodgepole saplings on the slope rising slowly to the mature forest. The near bank is more abrupt, a series of boulders and undercut trees holding back the stream. The little plants are less lush, lying two feet above the water. Upstream are five falls, each of at least a foot drop, some as much as three, freshening the water and spreading the sound. Downstream lie more falls, and more sound.

One of the bordering trees leans eight feet over the water before it straightens and rises forty feet vertically. The base is undercut more than half way, but the roots are so deep and robust that there is no possibility of their failure, of the tree falling to bridge the stream. And there is no need of a bridge, for a series of boulders spans the stream with secure steps. The sun passes over the far bank, making the wavelets glisten and glitter on their way around the rocks. The water sings a sprightly song, with syncopated bass burbles glooping from the upstream falls. It is noisy, but it is a calm and quiet noisy. And the water is clear and cold and clean, perfectly potable, as refreshing to the palate as it is to the ears and the eyes. Perfect.

The Perfect Forest is mature and clean. Most of the trees are fully grown, immune to the hazards of all but the fiercest of fires. Among them are a few younger trees, ready to assume the roles of their elders, to fill the gaps left by giants who fall, victims of wind or lightning or parasite. Many eager saplings sprout at their feet, hopeful of surviving the many, many hazards before them. Their chances are slim, slimmer than the saplings themselves, but some will survive. Some always survive.

There is thick brush at the skirts of the forest, rapidly thinning to near nothing in the unbroken shade within. A few grasses, an occasional flower, is all that accents the inner carpet of deep duff. Outcrops of bedrock, sometimes minor cliffs, hold the slope secure as the trees march upward to a wide flat, rolling away for many miles. Deer and elk and moose wander the woods, and foxes stalk field mice and squirrels and chipmunks. Robins and wrens and hatches and tits flirt through the branches, gobbling the insects who feed on decaying wood. The birds will sing, and the insects hum, but the rest maintain a respectful silence, except the squirrels, who have never understood the concept of respect. The forest is open, swept clean by periodic fires, a grassless lawn unmarred by paths or walkways.   The only trails are those made by the larger denizens to pick their way down the rocky hillside. It is a land of peace and plenty, kept so, ironically, by being of no commercial value.   The lodgepole pines are useless for structures, except as poles for lodges, and the soil cannot be plowed, cannot sustain a crop. Thus there is no temptation to "improve" the land nor to "put it to practical use". It will remain as it is, as it was, as it will be: Perfect.

The Perfect Campsite lies at the foot of the slope, by a creviced cliff of rock sixty feet wide and forty feet high, partly cloaked by the outlier trees of the Perfect Forest. A hundred feet from the cliff runs the Perfect Stream, and between them lies a wide and flat ground, high enough to be dry, shaded by several trees, one end cushioned by a perfect mattress of resilient duff, the other bare sand, perfect for a safe campfire. There is ample firewood nearby in the forest, and plenty of water to put the fire out. A deep pool by the near bank is perfect for storing bottles of drink, to keep it at the perfect temperature. At the tent site, the watersound is just loud enough. The fire site is at just the right place to catch a fish and have it cooking less than two minutes later. The trees mitigate the wind so it cannot ever be too strong, and shade is always present when it is wanted, yet it is sunny enough to heat a solar shower. There is no water runoff through the campsite, which is of less importance than it could be, for the weather is perfect for about six weeks of the year, and that is fine because I rarely stay as much as two weeks anywhere. I am sure it is far from being the only such campsite, but this one is better, because I know exactly where it is, and I can even get there on my bike. It cannot be improved and, God willing, no one will ever try. It will remain as it is: Perfect.

When Adam and Eve were expelled from Eden, an angel with a flaming sword was set to bar the entry. After a few thousand years, he went mad with boredom, and flailed about with his sacred sword, slashing Paradise into a thousand shards, then kicked them and scattered them throughout the world. He must have done so, for one of the fragments landed here.

Mountain Morning

Shepherd's dawn under a solid overcast. I light my morning fire, and the dim environs vanish as the leaping initial blaze consumes my night vision, and all I can see are the dancing flames, joyful at their liberation from their wooden cells, their sentences completed, freedom restored, though under parole to remain within the fire ring. Any coal violating the limits will be quickly arrested, swiftly suppressed, and crushed into the dust. The initial jubilance diminishes, and the freshly released flames dance upon the glowering glow of the coals. As their light ebbs, the light of the sky flows, the surrounding clouds become clear, and the sky, at last, becomes visible, the details becoming discernable.

The clouds are ominous. Though there is no break, there is not the uniform single mass of gray, but rather a congregation of dozens, perhaps hundreds, of jostling jumbles, thicker, thinner, darker, lighter, infinite shades of gray that fade imperceptibly together. Or change abruptly from one to another. The omen is rain, for this is the first summer after the breaking of the drought. There has been rain every week, so I am told, often every day. I was not here, but I know it to be true, for the land is green, and that is proof enough of the presence of plentiful water. This winter I watched a desert, a barren brown expanse of sand and stone become a grassy prairie, green and green where I had known only gray and brown. And now this familiar valley, these high meadows among the pines also retain their spring colors, in some places as rich as a pampered Beverly Hills lawn. That it will rain soon is very believable. But not certain, for these are mountain meadows, and mountain weather will do as it pleases, so you might as well just accept it. In an hour or two, the sky may be clear, or it may be snowing. In August. Mountains are like that. For now, the heralds proclaim rain. They promise rain, but it is a political promise, and may be forgotten or twisted in an instant.

The light grows, and the definition of clouds and trees and grass and gravel grow with it, smooth shapes gaining texture as their forms grow more solid. Several deer wander past, as they do every morning, young does and two young bucks, only two points on their antlers, still in velvet. The teens are on a date. Perhaps the bucks are hoping for an advantage, a head start on mating season. But the does are not ready. They may welcome the bucks' presence, but they will refuse their advances. Across the stream, two other bucks pass on their daily routine. Quite a different story, these mature males, eight or ten points each. They glance at the does, and you just know they are thinking "Soon, babe. Soon."

And in the sky appears a rift, a fuzzy patch, a hole, and it is full of blue. Instantly, with this one small change, the character of the entire sky changes. Suddenly, the clouds no longer mutter about rain. They say, in clear and sprightly voices, "Rain? *Us?* No, no, we do not bring *rain!* We are simply pretty pieces of scenery." And they break apart further, and deck themselves in pink and orange bunting as the rising sun clears their horizon, though it is still at least an hour below mine. A solid gray mass arises in the Southwest, but by the time it is overhead, its solidarity has shattered, it has become an array of individuals, and they, too, dwindle and evaporate as they approach the warming sun. Half of the sky says rain, the other half says shine. It is as dangerous as a modern American election, where you never know who will win, but certainly half of the people will lose, and will grumble their disappointment and disillusion. Hopefully only grumble.

But rain or shine, it will matter to me only in affecting my choice of activities. In the sun, I shall fend in the forest, gathering firewood for the week ahead, talking with the animals, walking with the trees, inhaling the air, feasting on the aromas of pine and duff and wildflowers. In the light rain, I shall wander the woods, gathering sticks and branches, seeking the silent spots where the fauna find haven from the wet, and splurging on the scents released by the damp. And if it rains hard, I shall sit in my tent and release my imagination, wandering with it, and writing what I find. I would prefer a dry overcast, because I would like to have a week's supply of wood on hand, in case of prolonged rain. But I will cheerfully take whatever weather comes, for I am an anarchist in weather as well as politics. Rules are okay, but the only one who rules, who makes decisions for me, is me.

The weather now is mild. The lack of recent rain means the creek has gone clear, so I can dip water from it to make a stew. There are no farms or fields upstream, so there are no fertilizers or pesticides in the runoff to contaminate the water. And, at this time, no mud. The air is chill, so the fire feels pleasant. I shall spend the morning here, warm and chill, a Baked Alaska morning anticipating a savory stew for lunch. I shall repair some gear, lazily industrious, in company with the trees, an object of curiosity to the deer and moose and robin and chipmunk, chatting with friends who wander by. There is nothing to desire, for everything is here. The stream and I laugh, for the sheer joy of being, because that is what we do.

So much for omens.

Why I Love the Mountains

Every part of the Wilds has its own beauty. The apparantly barren and lifeless desert bears a clean desolation, and ample wildlife, if you know when and where to look for it. Even truly barren and lifeless sand dunes boast an ever-changing graceful sinuosity and perfection of form. Grasslands hide an entire world within vast seas of seemingly nothing but simple stalks rippling in the wind. Foothills and high valleys and arctic tundra all harbor distinct eco-systems whose members thrive in their limited ranges, and swiftly succumb anywhere else. And glaciated peaks of bare rock that tower in lonesome and awesome grandeur, holding themselves above the teeming life-infested lands below. All of these are beautiful in their different ways, loved and loathed by different people for different reasons, like poker and polo, or banjoes and banana splits. Each is wonder-full and well worth a good long sojourn, long enough to experience it, to recognize it, to know it, to simply be it. Every person who knows these lands has his own favorite, for his own reasons. Mine is the

high montane, eight thousand feet and above, a bit lower in Idaho and Montana, a mite higher in Arizona and New Mexico. Why? Because to me, this land holds massive variety, can change its form, appearance, style in just a few feet. Walking or riding through this land satisfies a wanderlust of the mind as it satiates the wanderlust of the body. This land is special.

Early August in northern Wyoming is perhaps the best time and place of all. Certainly it is home to the best camp site in all the West, the only camp site for which I regularly make reservations. Here is one day that was typically unique: I awoke with the first light and entered the day. My first task was to light a fire, which I had laid the evening before. A touch of flame to the tinder, then off to my other chore, gathering ice from shallow pans laid out overnight. The ice filled a pair of gallon freezer bags, which lie in my cooler; I need not buy ice, when I can make my own. By the time I am done, the fire is well-caught, and warms my chilled hands rapidly. Feeling the bright radiance and deeply breathing the chill air is pleasing, comforting, the only sounds being the random pops and crackles of the glowing wood. There is no wind. The birds and bugs still sleep, waiting out the chill. A stick or two now and then keeps the blaze warm and bright. Cold water, icy cold, pumped by hand from a shallow well, pure and sweet and needing no chlorine or flavoring, counterpoints the heat. After an hour, the sun peeks out. Birds begin to chirp and sing as the chill breaks and fades in the light of the solar campfire. As the birds fare forth for the first sluggish insects, my fire has burned down to a bed of incandescent coals, and it is time for my breakfast, too. Pancakes, today.

As the sun rises, so does the wind. A gentle breeze at first, it will grow stronger along with the sunlight, for the light heats the hills to kindle convection currents. There are no clouds yet.

The air is still too cool, but the sunlight is already too warm, for at these altitudes, the air is thin, and does little to alleviate the burning power of the sun. I move to the shade, or semi-shade, a dappled spot where a ragged lodgepole blocks only half of the light. The wind sways the tree, so the segments of light move left and right, tempering the heat to a pleasant compromise. However hot the sun may become, however strong or weak the wind, the shade will provide, somewhere nearby, the perfect spot, the comfort zone. No matter what temperature I desire, at any moment, I will find it.

A pair of cranes fly by, and a deer wanders through the camp, gorging on lush green grass. He does not see me, for I do not move. He meanders about, a mouthful here, a nibble there, never too much, for the forest browsers are ardent conservationists; in the midst of abundance, they do not gorge at one spot, but partake of only a bit, never enough to begin to endanger a plant. He comes here every day, morning and evening, a regular customer of the Forest Buffet at the Buck Stop Diner. Dozens of butterflies flit among the dandelions, orange-brown wings with black spots, yellow wings with black trim.

As the buck departs, I take up my staff for a stroll among the spruce. A short hike up a twenty-five degree slope brings me to a long plateau, a sort of wide flat-topped ridge devoid of any trace of Man save a couple of sawn stumps. The trees are mostly lodgepole pine with a scattering of blue and white spruce. The ground is completely shaded, virtually devoid of undergrowth, and only six or eight saplings in sight at any time. It is cool enough to encourage a brisk pace, or as brisk as one can manage in the rarified air. I am long conditioned to it, but even so, it is easy to run out of breath. The breath-taking views contribute. There are a few standing snags, and many more fallen ones in various stages of decay. Some still bear bark, others are a uniform silver-gray like a well-weathered teak deck, and a few are simply long straight mounds that are only identifiable because I kniow they must be the last remains of an overthrown giant. There are few branches on the ground. That, and the tell-tale traces of weathered charcoal, bear quiet testimony to a fire in recent years. Perhaps wild, perhaps prescribed, the result is the same: A healthy and vigorous forest, almost like a park, so open that even the animals have made no trails. There is no need of them, one can walk anywhere unobstructed. Squirrels dash about, confident of their safety, chattering indignantly at the two-legged intruder. Birds sing among the needles, oblivious to my presence. The scent of spruce is strong, overpowering the pine perfume, though there are so many more of the massive pines. The duff is dry, so little of its aroma rises. At the edge of the ridge, the hill drops steeply to the vale below, the rim demarked by croppings and ledges of cracked and worn bedrock, washed clean of sand and tagged with lichen graffiti. I have read that lichen is a staple of the reindeer's diet, but see no sign that any of our mule deer have sampled it. The sharp slope becomes shallower, gentler, and a faint trace of a trail winds downward among a field of lichened boulders which seem to sprout like mushrooms from the loam. Too thin and faint for a footpath, I conjecture it was worn by deer and elk on their way to water. A brook sounds appealing, so I follow the trail cautiously. What is fair footing for a nimble and narrow-hoofed deer is a potential ankle-breaker for a big-footed two-leg. Grasses and meadow weeds start to spot the slope, and a faint feeling of moistness begins to pervade the atmosphere. Brush begins to crowd, and the trail becomes more pronounced, made obvious as a streak of nothing through low plants growing ever more lush, A quiet laughter drifts up from a sudden copse of long-leaf cottonwood, and there, through a pointed arch of leaves, appears the glimmering stream.

The bank of the brook is muddy, marked with many prints of tiny hooves. The trail continues on the other side, bordered by dense stands of cottonwood. Clearly, this is a safe watering hole, secured from ambush by the brush, if not from complete impassability, then by the impossibility of making a silent approach. The brush also renders the brook too obscured for a proper admiring of the cool flowing water, so I work my way downstream, expecting to find a more aesthetic scenic outlook. Sure enough, not too far below, a massive boulder ten feet high rests beside a short fall. I clamber atop and lie prone. I find to my surprise that this is the confluence of two streams, or perhaps it is one, which divided some way upstream, and the far bank is actually an island, an island twenty or forty times as broad as the stream in which it sits. Perhaps I shall explore upstream to find out. More likely I shall not, because it is of little significance. What matters is the view. A high stream to the right drops two or three feet into a half-pool, while a low stream to the left flows smoothly into the wash. Half of the flow turns in a gentle eddy, while the other half spins off into the distance, the short distance, for the channel bends out of sight only a score of feet away. A trout wags motionlessly beside the eddy, patiently waiting for food to come to him. Butterflies and bees seek nectar in the riparian flowers, blue and red and pink and purple. Something moves among the egg-sized pebbles; a salamander or a frog, a tadpole, an eft? I cannot tell, for it moves so swiftly and hides so well, and it is ten feet below me in any case. That is all right. I know it is there, and that is enough.

Enough. The sun is warm, but the stone is chill. I can return another day. I slip to the ground and wend my way down, forty feet from the water, where the ground is drier and the plants are sufficiently few that I can walk without crushing them at every step. I wish to leave as little trace of my passage as I can. I pause on a knoll, a small outcropping of rock, where

a break in the trees yields an unobstructed view of a wide open meadow, grass and shrubs and a seldom scattering of perfect blue spruce, exactly the shape and size likely to be selected for Christmas trees. But here, no one will harvest them. With luck, they will grow tall, and their progeny will slowly fill the meadow. Or perhaps not. There are rocks in the meadow, boulders or bedrock, I cannot tell from here. It may be that the soil is too sparse, too shallow for trees, and that would explain why there is a meadow here at all. A fox trots leisurely from one side to the other, not hunting, heading homeward. I know this fox, a vixen with a brace of kits. No doubt it is the little ones' dinnertime.

Ahead is a distinctive outcropping silhouetted on the ridgeline. I can see it from my camp, some three miles to the westnorthwest. I am only a half mile from home, over that way. But there is a ridge in the way, so I will have to walk more than a mile further through the woods. On the other hand, there is a ridge in the way, so I get to walk more than a mile further through the woods! Out here, there is no rush, no hurry. I have nothing better to do, for there *is* nothing better to do. I laugh, for the sheer happiness of being here.

Eventually, in my own good time, I return to camp, where I lunch on bannock bread I baked this morning, with honey and butter and just a touch of cinnamon, washed down with freshly pumped well water. No restaurant in the world, not even a crowded truck stop, ever served so delicious a dinner. For one thing, they cannot provide an appetite to compare with one built from the walk and the woods and the virgin mountain air.

I sit and do nothing, just be there, an integral part of the whole wild world. Songbirds flock to glean the scattered crumbs. Chipmunks condemn me for eating everything, not paying the tax they impose on all campers. I simply smile at the greedy thieves, already fat from the bribes they extort, and from the scraps they steal. Say rather the choice viands they make off with, leaving only scraps of the food they have ruined in their reckless greed.

The warm sun drowses me, and I drift away, perhaps dreaming, but I can not always differentiate between this waking life and a fantasy dream. For I am living the dream that so many share, but cannot live themselves because they will not cut loose from the anchors that hold them back. They could; the restraints are all self-imposed. But for whatever reason, be it fear, confusion, ignorance, or even a sense of duty, they hold on. For some, it is the right decision; for some, this life would be a betrayal, or a torment. But for many, it would be a culmination, a fulfillment; but they will only dream, and sigh, and regret, and envy. Pity.

And now the sun descends. The temperature, which peaked in the eighties, is slowly sliding towards its freezing nadir just before the dawn. It is time to think of supper, and to lay the morning fire and fill pans with water to, hopefully, freeze. Or perhaps I shall have an evening fire, to lose myself in flickering flames, to watch it evolve into embers, then turn my gaze on the sky full of stars. The nearest villages, only a few hundred inhabitants each, lie thirty miles away, and four thousand feet below. There are no settlements on this high plateau. The sky is clear and dry, with no haze to catch the loom of light, what little there is from the distant tiny villages. Between the lack of light and the tenuous atmosphere, the stars sparkle little, and blaze with a brilliance unimaginable to those poor unfortunates who only see the sky from towns, or think they see it from cities.

But I might not watch it tonight, for it will probably be equally stupendous tomorrow, and certainly several times during the next week or two. It is not a seldom sight in the montane zone; it is the usual, the normal, the common, though never commonplace.

And this is the glory of the perfect places. Today I saw so much, so many things so different, so wonderful. It was nothing unusual, nothing special, nothing remarkable. It was the usual special occurences one can remark almost every day, if one will only look. This is why I love the montane in summer. It is unique, with such wide ranges of everything that almost every thing can be found here every week. Cold and hot, wet and dry, light and dark, life and death, every thing I could desire. Here are companions to share it with, and solitude to keep it all to myself. Here I can be by myself or accompanied by wild friends or by human friends. Here I can loaf and do nothing, or be industrious and walk or write or dream or ride. Here I can be cause or effect, or both at once. And here every day is the same, in that each is different, and I never know what will happen, and always know that each occurence will be new and familiar and fascinating and fun. Here I am happy. Here I am fulfilled.

Perfection Plus

Last year I proclaimed this to be the perfect campsite. Today I tell you that even perfection can be improved.

There has been more rain this Spring and Summer. More importantly, the rain has been slow and steady, not just the occasional thunderstorm, the downpour that soaks the surface and rushes off to stain the creek and rivers brown. Slow, steady, heavy drizzle that lasts for eight, ten, twelve hours, saturating the surface, seeping through the duff, soaking into the ground. The soil and the roots of the surface plants are always moist. The moisture has reached the deeper dirt, where the roots of the giant trees anchor the massive trunks, and drink what water they can find, water that is now abundant. The seepage has penetrated to the aquifer, raising the water table. The cast iron pump, source of such delectable water, last year required eleven strokes to start the splendid beverage flowing. Now it only needs eight. The temperature is the same. The air is the same. The sunlight is the same, though there may be less overall because of the additional clouds. Only the water has changed. But that is enough. That is all that was needed.

There were flowers here before. They lined the creek, a colorful border for the crystal clear water. The riparian weeds were lush, deep green, their roots submerged and their fronds trailing in the flow. But now their lushness extends many feet from the creek, and their stems stand in the water, for the water is deeper, only five or six inches more, but also half again last year's level. The flowers extend with the lushness. The bit of meadow adjacent to the camp was rich golden grass gone to seed. It is in seed again, but taller, thicker, and still green. It is infested with flowers, every square foot, white and red and blue and orange and purple and yellow. I can see flowers in every direction I look except straight up, and even there, many of the trees are still, or again, in flower. Half-way through August, Spring still lingers.

The meadow across the creek puts this little bit to shame. Not only is the clearing many times larger, the grass is taller, the bracken thicker, the blossoms larger and brighter, the colors more intense. In this case it is true, the grass on the other side *is* greener. Tastier, too, and more nutritious. So the deer tell me as they gratefully graze twice a day, morning and evening. And there are so many more of them. Last year I was lucky to see four all day. This morning I had been visited by eight before the first sunlight touched the trees. I cannot conceive the population has increased so much in so short a time. I must attribute it to the largesse of succulent browse free for the taking. Perhaps the animals believe the abundance is of our doing (we do, after all, produce incredibly delicious crops in our farmland), and, knowing two-legs ooh and ahh to see them, they are displaying themselves to show their gratitude.

Every thing is more than last year, even the trees, for the adults are greener, their foliage thicker, and the seedlings sprout in the field like kindergarteners on a, pardon me, field trip. More grass, more flowers, more animals, more birds, more creek, more watersound. Even elk half way across the great meadow, of which they normally inhabit only the fringes, and moose wandering in the middle of the campground itself. More of everything, and larger, and richer.

But there is one other factor that so greatly enhances the Perfect Campsite. Last year it was occupied by others. I could only visit it, look upon it like a child on the sidewalk, gazing at the marvels in the toy store window. Today it is mine. My bike is parked under a tree, my tent is pitched on the plain, my stew is simmering on my fire. For two weeks I shall inhabit this paradise, I shall immerse myself in the beauty and peace and perfection. I can rarely tolerate staying as much as two weeks in one camp, but here I could stay four, and would, if it was allowed. Oh, well, I can always look at it as sharing.

Now, I do not wish to seem greedy, but looking at how this perfection has improved, I cannot help but wonder: If these conditions continue, what will this site be like next year?

Sinks Canyon

Wyoming

Why Go On?

It was seven hundred miles from Here to There, so I split the trip into two stages. But shortly before departure, a friend described The Sinks as a place I should visit, some day. Now, I usually place little value on recommendations such as that, because there are so many many places that I should visit, some day, that I could not visit them all in half a millenium. I just make a note, and rarely change my plans to detour to one of them. I include some in plans for future trips, but mainly do not go sooner unless one happens to lie along my path. As it happens, though, in this case The Sinks lay along my route, about a third of the way along, so I decided to stop there for a short rest along the way. It would only be ten miles out of my way, adding perhaps an hour to the day's travel time, and if I liked it, why, I could stay overnight, breaking my trip into three stages instead of two. It would mean reaching There on

Wednesday instead of Tuesday, which would still be soon enough to assure me a site over the Labor Day weekend. So I detoured to The Sinks for a short stop. It was fine, very fine. I decided to stay overnight. The weather was warm, and all of the signs indicated no rain tonight. No need to pitch the tent; a sleeping bag would suffice. I could rise early in the morning and be on the road in half an hour. Nine hours on the road would see me to There. Nine hours of travel.

"Travel" and "travail" sound very similar. One vowel change and a shift of emphasis, but their meanings are so different, completely unrelated. But it was not always so. At one time, their pronunciations were identical, and so were their definitions, for they were the same one word, and travel *was* travail. Difficult, dangerous and daunting, a journey was a thing only for the strong, hemmed in by hazards, which few would undertake, and none without great need. Indeed, times have changed, and yet, not completely. There is a term in the biker community, "ironbutt". It denotes a person who has ridden at least five hundred miles in a single day. If one averages fifty MPH, including stops for gas, that means ten hours in the saddle. Equestrians understand the difficulty of this. They will tell you, if, after a day of riding, your legs hurt, then your stirrups are too short. If your butt hurts, your stirrups are too long. If both hurt, they are just right. See why five hundred miles merits the name "ironbutt"? There is still some travail in travel. So tomorrow, instead of a nine-hour leg, I will likely only do half. More or less.

I woke a bit after midnight. As I slept, the few clouds had abandoned the sky. A light breeze was blowing, but it was a warm breeze. The sky was largely dark, about a Bortle Class 4 to the Northeast, brightened by the loom of Lander some ten miles away, but a good Class 3 to the Southwest. All of the stars of the Little Dipper were clearly visible, and the Milky Way flowed brightly across the sky. It was a wonderful, enchanting view, and I gazed at it between drowses all of the rest of the night.

A few bits of wispyness have drifted before the stars, and the dimmer ones are departing. In the East, Venus brightly bares her beauty long after the rest of the celestial host have faded to nothing. A faint pinkness appears where the sky and the earth meet, and slowly, imperceptibly slowly, grows and expands. A cloud forms a few degrees above the horizon and drinks the glow, enhancing it, enlarging it, my morning fire kindled in the sky, since I have no need of it here in camp. Nature is so considerate, such a perfect hostess. As the skylight grows, the northern cliffs resolve from the gloom, taking on first shape, then detail,then color. Venus fades to the merest prick, barely visible, but there if you know where to look. The clouds catch fire and spread their incandescence across the sky. The cliff tops burst into flame, and the flames flow silently to the talus and brush below. In a sudden burst of glory, the sun emerges from nocturnal obscurity, and the world glows its gratitude, a warm welcome for the Lord of Light.

As I listen to the subdued rush of wind in the pines, and the rumble of the river rushing over rocks, I know there will be no travail today. Just a short trip to town for some provisions. About a week's worth.

Middle Popo Agie

I would like to tell you about a different place.   Not unique or peculiar or magnificent or wonderful. Not necessarily. Of all of the lone adjectives that would fit, "different" is the most significant. It is the watershed of the Middle Popo Agie River. That is the old Indian name (except "middle", which has been translated).   It was almost certainly first written down by a Frenchman, because the name is pronounced "Po-POH-shue" or "Po-POH-shui"; only the French can misspell that badly.

The Middle Popo Agie is not a major river, not significant or useful or practical. It is not navigable, and provides little irrigation. Even so, it is a treasure of great value, real value, of worth far beyond the merely practical or commercial. It cannot be bought or matched by any amount of money, nor is it worth even a single cent. The river and its watershed are simply not related to money, just as altitude is not related to music.

We pick up on the Middle Popo Agie where it passes through the town of Lander. It is a substantial river, big enough to swim in, big enough for boating, clearly more, much more than a mere creek, and mostly too wide and deep to ford. We follow it southwest, upstream, past a rapidly dwindling number of houses and, after just a few miles, enter broken country. Very broken, more vertical than flat. In fact, if you were to start just seven miles northwest of this point, and travel a straight line to here, you would have to cross no fewer than eleven gulches, each with a flowing creek, only one of them intermittent. It would take you at least two days to do so, for unless you are an expert rock climber, you would have to hike a good thirty miles to stay anywhere near the straight-line course. Steep, broken, rocky. This land is *rough*. And after all of this pain and struggle and travail, you would reach a river, a wide and often raging river, which you could stroll across without getting your feet wet, without even realizing you were crossing the river at all! Different. Because, about a mile later, about eight miles from town, we come to the beautiful Rise of the Popo Agie.

The Rise is a great hole in the ground, a good twenty feet across, from which a river swells and rises from the Stygian darkness to flow under the light of day. That is a pretty good statement, accurate, nicely poetic, and completely misleading, because the picture it invokes does not match reality at all.

What the Rise looks like is a quiet and clean, sandy pond, long and rather narrow, filled, packed, even, with trout, some as much as ten or twelve pounds. This is a haven for them, a safe space, because no fishing is allowed till the river passes under the road. The trout, mostly Brown and Rainbow, have worked their way up the river, perhaps for spawning, perhaps simply wandering. I suspect they have a natural tendency to swim upstream when they can; they tend to face into the current, and rarely swim backwards. Once they arrive in the Rise, they have little reason to leave. It is clean, with a constant strong flow of fresh and clear water, perfectly filtered by the sand bed through which it has risen, a constant, never-ending flow which prevents the pond from freezing up even in the coldest winter. There are many fish here, but there is ample food. It falls from the sky, manna from heaven, in the form of vitamin-packed pellets, bread and bagels, tossed in by the gawking two-legs tourists. And there are rarely any predators; the constant flow of people discourages their approach.

If you look carefully at the northern shore, at the base of a looming cliff, you can spot eight or ten springs, tiny rivulets emerging from the sand and gravel, each one producing no more water than you would get from a household faucet.

But then you look east and see the outflow. There is a good two hundred cubic feet pouring out of the pond every second. A thousand springs of the size you can see would not provide so much water. And yet it flows. It must come from somewhere. See the sandbar in the middle of the pond? It is soaking wet. The sand spit above it, the one with springs on either side, is dry. Why? Because the entire bed of the pond, the whole bed, is a spring. You cannot see it, but there is water flowing up through the sand, through *all* of the sand. And it is bringing more sand with it. The sand bars grow all summer and fall, then wash away in the spring flood.

This is the point where the Popo Agie rises, but it is not the source of the river. Nope. Go on past the Rise. Wander up the valley. You cannot see the river, but you are walking on it. Or above it. You cannot even hear it behind you, for it is not noisy. There is no trace of the river, except the canyon itself.

To the right the canyon wall towers over its steep talus footing, thick with pines and firs that conceal the shattered stones that fall from the cliffs every year, pinballing among the trees and sometimes felling the smaller ones, occasionally uprooting a giant patriarch.

To the left stands the same cliff, or rather, the same strata through which the river has chewed its way for millions of years. Instead of trees, it is cloaked in sagebrush, creosote and bunchgrass; there are no trees for the tumblerocks to take down.

Looking back, you might expect a river to course along the south side. You would almost be correct. Often, during the great spring thaw, the river is four or five times its usual size, two million cubic feet per hour or more. It is too much for the secret underground passages, and the excess becomes a river

of its own, a second level, an elevated spillway. How many rivers of the world flow on two levels? Well, probably a lot of them, but this one you can see! Right over there, the boulder-strewn bed of a dry river. That is the Upper Middle Popo Agie River. And after a bit, ahead  of you as well. It is only a quarter mile or so till you can see the cave, a big hole more or less clogged with driftwood, and the whole river pouring into it and vanishing without a trace. These are the Sinks of the Popo Agie, for it is the same river. It was proven, years ago, by adding chemical markers to the waters above the Sinks. Soon the markers were detected in the Rise. Well, not *soon*.

The water's path between the Sinks and the Rise is odd, very odd. The river is flowing a good three or four miles per hour, so it only takes it about four or five minutes to traverse a quarter mile. Naturally, we would expect the water flow to be somewhat slower underground, having to work through many small channels and gaps between the rocks. But it took the markers some three to five hours to appear in the Rise. The volume of water coming out of the Rise is also much greater than the volume flowing in, so there is at least one more tributary or spring joining the river underground, but *five hours?* That is less than two percent of the speed of the surface river. A few years ago, a couple of scuba divers went in to see if they could find out anything. We do not know if they did or not; they have yet to come back out. (Actually, that is only legend. Wyoming folk have a tendency to, ah, tell stretchers.)

But the river above the Sinks is Different. The Sinks (and the Rise) lie in the Sinks Canyon State Park, just a few miles long. The Park ends where the Shoshone National Forest begins, with the Sinks Canyon campground. Above this campground is a picnic area and a National Forest work center, just a building where maintenance crews store their tools. Nothing else. No campgrounds, no toilets, no buildings. No houses, no farms or fields, no pastures, not even open range. The river here is pure. You can drink directly from it. Well, *I* can. If you have a weak, unexercised immune system that has never had to deal with water that did not come out of a bottle, you might get sick. You would be equally likely to get sick from drinking tapwater in a city other than your home. This water is clear. There is nothing upstream to contaminate it, not even a road. There might be a dead animal decaying in the water There are probably several, mice, squirrels, fish. But they vanish quickly, consumed by scavengers, and the way this water is bouncing and flowing and aerating itself in the rapids and falls, it is purified very quickly. The Forest Service will warn you to not drink the water without treating it. They have to. If some weak-bellied city-dweller drank it and got sick, there would be a lawsuit, and in our demented society, the Forest Service would lose. So I tell you, you can drink this pure, clear water untreated, but only at your own risk. *I* will not get sick. You might.

It is here, where the waters are pure and the last tokens of civilization peter out, that the story actually begins. Though only fifteen miles from its furthest source (and there are scores of springs, each being a source, a part of the headwaters), here the river is already almost halfway to the sea. For here, the elevation is only 6,850 feet, and the highest source is on Wind

River Peak, which towers to 13,192 feet. The waters have dropped over a mile, and have a mile and a quarter left to fall, but they have flowed only fifteen miles, and yet have eighteen hundred still ahead. A short distance upstream thunder the Popo Agie Falls, and four miles beyond them begins the Popo Agie Wilderness. The river and its many tributary creeks permeate this portion of the wilderness area, right up to the Continental Divide (the waters that spring forth just five miles farther west flow down the other side of the mountain range, and need cross only half of the distance to reach the sea), and this watershed, with an area of less than eighty square miles, contains more than eighty lakes, and also a thing which most people would never imagine could exist in such mountainous

terrain, at such high altitude. At nine, ten, eleven thousand feet, one expects cliffs and crags, steep slopes, vertical acres, swift rapids and many tumultuous cascades. And one does indeed find them here. But there must be flat plains and sluggish shallow streams to allow marshes to form. What, do *they* exist in this high montane? Yep. They surely do. Right over there. Acres and acres of soggy marsh, and more acres of sunny meadows. For the western slopes of the Wind River Mountain Range are much less precipitous than this eastern side, ten or fifteen miles north of the legendary South Pass, but there is a lot of flat plateau before the sudden plunge begins.

The Pass was described to the fur trappers, the mountain men, as "the pass that does not look like a pass", and "a long, treeless valley". Different from other passes, as this wilderness is different from other wildernesses, and this river is different from other rivers. Indeed, different from everywhere. I have seen no place that resembles this one more than remotely. I have seen cliffs like these, but never near a river like this. I have seen rivers like this, but never in a canyon like this. I have seen rises like this, but with no sinks. I have seen nothing like the Sinks. In fact, there is little that I have seen elsewhere that is not represented here, in small. Bear's Tepee. An active volcano. Geysers. That is about all.

Perhaps this is where all of the scraps and shavings, the leftover bits and pieces were stored after the creation of the rest of the world.   Or perhaps it is the prototype, the test bed or the

scale model made to prove the concepts before building the full scale planet. Either way, it is a fine showcase. If you are fit, and enjoy multi-day hikes on not-easy trails, you will have a fine time here. If you are not, you can spend several days strolling along the lower river (for there are easy trails, too) or just sitting in the quiet. There is a lot of quiet here. You might meet up with me while you are loafing, for I shall surely return.

La Posa

Arizona

Greetings

It is a wonderful thing to have friends, old friends. Most are wanderers like me, and we know we'll meet again, don't know where, don't know when, but we know we'll meet again some sunny day. I usually don't expect it, but am never surprised, when I stop at some campground and find them there. I like to go to places where I have not been before. When I arrive at a new campground, I make a slow circuit, looking over all of the sites, finding which is the best, and which unoccupied one is best. Usually they are the same site, for I am lucky, and often the features I seek are different from the ones the short-term campers value. But it is not at all uncommon to be greeted by old friends. "Hi, Lone! Come on over when you're settled!" I wave back, or just toss my head, if the road is rough or rutted. After all, I am on a loaded bike, moving slowly. I am not about to take my hands off of the controls! Sometimes I am greeted more than once, especially in places where I am returning, for I also get to know the camp hosts, and most of them return to the same campground year after year. I once pulled into Rueter Campground, up by Bear's Tepee, and "Hi, Lone!". "Hi, Lone." "Hey, Lone, good to see you." I was greeted twice, then greeted by the host, then greeted by two more before pulling into my favorite site. (It is clearly the best site, but oddly, it has always been open every time I have been there.) While I was setting up, not half an hour later, another group pulled in and selected the site just after mine, "Hi, Lone! We're neighbors!" Every person in that campground was an old friend. Only one of them, Ray's new girlfriend, was an old

friend I had not met before. (There are a lot of them, too.)
When I am greeted on arrival, it is like coming home. Indeed,
it *is* coming home, even in a place where I have never before
been. Home has nothing to do with hanging hats, or ancestors,
or birthplaces, or growing up. Home is not memories of places
or things or even times. Home is where one is known. Home
is where friends are.

Sometimes the animals greet me. Ravens remember, and
sometimes other birds, and rabbits, and even squirrels. Yes,
even those vacuum-skulls can remember some things, if they
are drummed into their heads, and concern food. Or danger. I
do not throw most food scraps in the trash. Instead, I scatter
them for the wildlife. Except in bear country. You do *not* want
to entice bears, not at all, at all! But the birds love bits of bread
crusts, and rabbits grow ecstatic over carrot tops and especially
cabbage leaves. And anything not eaten decays and returns to
the soil. When I pull into my favorite site at Upper Tonto
Creek, the ravens come and greet me, and watch me set up
camp. At Burnt Corral, by the time my tent is pitched, at least
a couple of cardinals are in attendance, talking to me.

Sometimes the mountains and streams and trees welcome
me back. The mountains look down with approval, the streams
chuckle "Hi, Lone!", the trees wave. Yes, I know they are
simply reflecting my own recognition and appreciation of
them, that their greetings are nothing more than my own
remembrance of earlier times. Probably. But the pleasure is no
less real, and they are old friends, regardless of how others may
scoff. The forest greets me. That is all that matters.

But sometimes I am less sure. Sometimes coincidence
seems even more unlikely than intent.

I returned to Quartzsite after a long and wonderful year
touring Utah, and Idaho, and Montana, and Wyoming, and the

Dakotas. I even passed through Colorado, which becomes more disappointing every year. I spent a marvelous autumn in New Mexico, and found there a new winter home. But I had to return to La Posa, at least for a few weeks. I had spent last winter there, my first, after California became unacceptable. It is difficult, even painful, to stay at one place for months, even a place like La Posa. It is a beautiful place, with usually very good weather, rarely even freezing, many old friends, and the finest sunrises and sunsets in the world. No, not just "the finest I have seen". The finest. Period. I have seen many, in many far countries, and in many near lands. Some are truly breath-taking, some are vastly impressive, such as the sunsets seen from a hundred miles east of Los Angeles, when the light of the setting sun shatters in the smog and blazons the clouds with blazes of color. "Spielberg sunsets", we called them. But the grandest of them all were only on a par with the typical common sunsets of Quartzsite. And when Quartzsite decides to let herself go, to exert an extra effort to produce an all-out solar spectacular. . .

Truly, in all the world, there is nothing to compare, except possibly a beautiful girl.

So I returned to Quartzsite, to La Posa, for a couple of weeks or so. I cruised down Main Street, slowly, refreshing memories of which stores were the best, then leisurely south, relaxing after the long high-speed run along the Interstate. I made the turn into La Posa South, grinding over the gravel path to the area my friends occupied. But there were none to be seen. A stranger occupied the site I had used, and I stopped just beyond, where another friend had been, but was not. I dismounted and cleared the larger rocks from a space for my tent. and began to set up camp. As I laid out the tent, my neighbor, an old friend I was just meeting, came over. As we chatted an old friend from last year walked up. "Hi, Lone! Good to see you!" Another arrived. "Hey, Lone, where have you been?" A car drove by, and the driver waved. "Lone! Hey, Lone!" And another. "Hey, Lone, you're late!"

After pitching the tent and stowing my gear, I strolled through the brush and rocks. I came to the site where we were accustomed to gather, and old friends were there. We shook hands and clapped shoulders and hugged and petted and licked. (No, it's not like that! Some of my old friends are dogs.) I sat, and more friends drifted in. And more. And we talked, and told where we had been and what we had done, and what we had seen, and found, and learned. We talked the afternoon away, happy to see each other and be together once again. And the day waned, and the sun set.

"The sun set." That statement is about as inadequate as "the hydrogen bomb exploded".

The clouds were perfect. The air was clear. The view was unobstructed. The sun set. I can only begin to describe it, for words cannot approach doing justice to a sight beyond mortal experience. The high clouds covered the western half of the sky and the sun made a sable silhouette of the jagged mountains as it settled behind them, the sky turning a brilliant glowing red and neon orange that spanned from ground to zenith and flowed around the entire horizon, and literally every degree was colored red and deep pink in a full and unbroken circle of beauty. The sky became a scarlet crown encircling the land, and the forepiece blazed almost too bright to gaze upon, as the Quartzsite Sunset declared herself Queen of the Skies, Empress of the Esthetic, the definitive definition and embodiment of Beauty, unmatched, *unapproached*, for She is the Mother of Glory!

For a full half hour, we were gods. We had to be, for the sight, even the mere memory, of such magnificence was more than enough to strike any mortal dead. Even the last fading minutes of the celestial spectacular were the equal of any other sunset at any other place. We were all in agreement: No finer, no grander sunset had ever been seen, even here.

Quartzsite had said, "Hi, Lone!"

First Dawn, Second Dawn

Back on the Bad Old Days, when I lived in a city, I often did not want to get up in the mornings. Having a Schedule, being required to be in a certain place at a certain time, meant waking by a certain time, and if I was short of sleep, well, that was just too bad. It is also unhealthy. I would treasure those days when I had no schedule, when I could lie in bed all day if I so chose. But there were always many things I wanted to do in my precious free time, things important to me, if perhaps to no one else, so I would get up, but maybe after enjoying a sybaritic hour of "wasting" time; it was my day, and I could do as I pleased. But these are the Good New Days. I still have a schedule, but it does not include time, just things I want (or need) to do, and can do when I choose to do them. And I find that, with a perverseness almost as great as that of the universe, it is a very rare day when I am not up before the sun. And therein lies a serendipitous reward, especially in Quartzsite.

Quartzsite, as I have noted elsewhere, is a peculiar place, especially in the celestial arena. Her sunsets are legendary and widely acknowledged, and her sunrises are just as good. But a special peculiarity, almost a uniqueness, are her dawns. Dawns begin with the first light, Shepherd's Dawn, when a white thread (originally, a goat hair) can first be distinguished from a black one, and continue to a blazing peak as the first limb of the sun peeks over the horizon . . . except in Quartzsite.

I arose this morning, as usual before the faintest lightening of the night. The sky was nearly clear, only a shallow fringe of clouds around the edges, a tonsure typical of, almost unique to, the La Posa Plateau. It does not obscure any stars, for as grand as it is, the night sky here is never better than a Bortle Class Four; the looms of Yuma, Phoenix, and Southern California are as bright as the Milky Way, and Quartzsite itself not only looms, but the lamps themselves are visible. Unless I interpose my tent between us. If there were a power failure out here on the scale of the Great New England Blackout, the sky would be magnificent. But the blackout would have to extend over two hundred miles in every direction, maybe more. As it is now, for most of the sky, the dimmer stars are drowned out; the Pole Star is visible, but the other components of Ursa Minor might as well not exist. Orion is, of course, supremely prominent, and all of the Twins and the Bull are visible. The Pleiades and the Andromeda Nebula can be discerned, and make a good showing in binoculars or a telescope. If the objects you seek are in the middle, darker part of the sky, naked-eye stargazing is a wonderful way to start a day, especially in October and November, when the dawning is in cool contrast to the ninety-degree afternoons. But after an hour or so, the stars begin to fade away. It is the beginning of the dawns.

The loom of Phoenix lies in the East, a perpetual false dawn that appears at sunset and never varies all night long, except when there are clouds over the city, clouds that enhance the glow. But in a prelude to the dawn, the loom seems to grow and swell, pregnant with the embryo of the new day. Gradually, the glow expands, encroaching on the firmament, swallowing stars and galaxies, erasing the universe, making it a palimpsest to record the newly borning hours. "Let there be light!" resounds silently through the world, and Night slinks off sullenly, spitefully, to the West. A slight tint of color, a light hint of pink, tentatively touches the bases of the lowest clouds. Slowly, almost invisibly, yet speeding at nearly nine hundred miles per hour, the new hue reaches out from the still-hidden sun, gracing and glazing the atmospheric lakes with rose and cherry, the pale bodies becoming sun-burned, a deep, almost bottomless red, spreading like a tide, a red tide, across the entire expanse till half of the eastern sky revels in the First Dawn. And then it fades. As slowly as it grew, the color dwindles, the burn heals, and the tonsure ages to pale gray, stark against the blue-gray sky. The last touch of pink washes away and vanishes. It is over. Finished. Done.

This is the true False Dawn, a preliminary lightening of the sky which then fades away. I see it almost everywhere, but I have yet to see the presage of colors anywhere except La Posa. At its best, it is almost the equal of some true dawns I have seen, so much so that in La Posa, I prefer to call it First Dawn. But that is only the overture; the rest of the symphony continues. Now there is a Second Dawn, the True Dawn. Now the color returns, the clouds begin to pink and redden anew. It is faster, much faster, and the palette is not exhausted when the clouds are deep red. The paint ignites, it gleams, it brightens into fiery orange, with sparks of yellow, streaks of light, delightful borders delineating different clouds, rows and flows of cotton clouds, each level, each angle a different hue, dull and sullen red superimposed on glaring flares of brilliant gold and ebony shadow, forming fantastic shapes of unimaginable castles and beasts, dragons and towers, cliffs, rivers, waterfalls, in a senseless and planless plethora of images and ideas, an abstract of infinite colors, and changing with every instant, growing, glowing, brightening, expanding to fill the heavens, the Face of God surveying the newly created land. And a brilliant spark appears in a notch in the farthest ridgeline, the first glimpse of the sun as the day is finally, after a bright and dramatic labor, born. The glorious light pours from the rising orb, too bright to be seen, burning the colors from the clouds to leave them white-hot and pristine, purified and cleansed of every taint of pollution. We are presented with a divine gift, a new day, fresh, unsullied, free of any flaw, to do with however we please. Its potentials are without limit. We can create, or destroy, anything we choose. We can make it a day of honor or of sin, of Heaven or of Hell, of creation or of destruction, a day to remember forever, or to strive to forget. *Any* thing.

So, what shall we do to day?

Blown Away

The strongest winds I have experienced since the last time I had to ride through a hurricane in the Caribbean are not in the mountains, where most people would expect them. A winter storm at ten thousand feet is a terrible thing, an awful thing, possibly even horrible. Sixty, seventy, eighty mile an hour winds, unobstructed by any impediment strike the unyielding mountainside and swirl among the crags and clefts, twisting into vortices that are miniature tornados, stationary spirals that destroy nothing only because there is nothing to destroy. That pretty little lea lies there because that is where the spinning devil dances during every storm; any sapling so luckless as to root in it is evicted before April, ripped off of the mountain and spun into a valley a mile away and a mile below. Any bold adventurer so foolish as to camp in that spot would surely do the same. But, while I will concede that I am a fool, I am not foolish north-northwest. When the wild winter winds are skiing among the alps, I am in the South, in the low desert, in the dry sand, enduring balmy breezes and warm winds, gentle things, five or seven knots, temperatures in the seventies on the Winter Solstice, nights only rarely descending to freezing.

Usually.

It is midnight of the longest night. Dawn will bring the sacred Solstice, the sun touching the peaks as far south as it ever lies. I look forward to it, but today I may not see it, because the Wind is here. Not that it is dangerous, not to me. But the dust...

The air was still this morning. Smoke from my cookfire rose straight and true.   My hummingbird neighbor flitted around, sipping from his feeder and curiously observing my inexplicable two-legs antics. (We are a source of inexhaustible amusement for these infinitely inquisitive birds.) The usual morning breeze began, gradually growing as it often does, and by noon, it still was barely enough to stir the dust. But it continued to build, to strengthen. Soon I had to tighten my chin-strap, lest my hat go walkabout on its own. Gusts became intrusive, eyes began to itch, the distant mountains began to soften. The dust was rising. Loose papers and a couple of light grocery bags kited from the South, tangling in the brush to buzz in the wind, the strengthening wind. Up came the blue bandana, as I hid my face from the wind. If the storm does not notice me, perhaps it will go away.

With the dusk, I retreated to my tent. It cannot keep the dust out, but it does slow it down. Nothing blows into my eyes, though it settles in the relatively still air, settles on everything, everywhere. The winds are strong, thirty or forty miles per hour, and gusting to fifty, sixty, maybe more, and growing stronger. I recall the times when I used commercial plastic tents; such a toy would be lying flat tonight, a reed before the wind. But I now dwell in a real tent, a solid canvas tent, with strong manila guy lines, two to each corner. There is nothing weak or flimsy about it, and there is nothing about it that will degrade in the unremitting desert sunlight. This tent has stood before sixty and seventy mile winds before. I have confidence. It is an oak. But while I am sure it will stand, I also know it will flap and rattle. Sleep may not be so solid tonight, so I retire early. And it is well that I do, for the gusts continue, and grow stronger, and sleep is fitful. I rise from semi-slumber with the impression of a memory of a crunching crash. Again, to a rattling, syncopated drumming. And again, suspecting there was a deep and dull thump from somewhere upwind. Mostly, though, the sound is simply the flutter of canvas, the muffled whip-crack one hears when shaking out a blanket. I have pondered long and hard, but never invented a means of silencing the tent, only mitigating the noise by use of taut guy-lines. But no matter. I have fourteen hours to get enough sleep.

And now it is midnight. In seven hours I have slept perhaps four. I feel rested, awake, alert, so I rise to investigate. I must walk carefully, and often stagger, for the wind still blows, still gusts. A flashlight is of little use, for the dust is like a fog, thick, brown, devouring the beam before it has shone forty feet. The sky may hold a solid overcast, or be bereft of even a single cloud, but I cannot tell, for the dust overhead is thick; I see no stars, and the moon is not yet up. My guys are still firm, but I tighten a few, taking out the slack which a gusting wind always produces. The bushes to the North are festooned with plastic bags, Holiday trimmings just in time for Christmas. Boxes are piled at their bases, but instead of gaily wrapped presents, they arc only cmpty cartons rolled from the broad plain to the South. This is La Posa in December, and there are thousands, tens, even hundreds of thousands of RVs around me, and many are new, and do not know the Boojum wind, do not know that anything left out may softly and silently vanish away. Few are in sight, for most are encamped to the North and West, and the camping grounds are many square miles in extent. And now, the dust and the dark cut visibility to the next thing to nothing. That is the Desert: You can see forever, or fornever. The lights of Quartzsite, always shining brightly over a few miles of space, are only a glow, and a weak one at that. The ubiquitous fireflies of solar-powered nightlights, dearly beloved by the resident wanderers, are snuffed, dimmed to nothing by the wandering land. One light alone crawls despairingly to me, struggling painfully fully half a hundred feet; my neighbor, wakened by the waggling of his van, reads to pass the time.

As I stood here, seeing what could be seen, and what could not, feeling the wind, the flying sand, knowing the night, as I stood here, the wind changed. It was not abrupt, it took a minute or two, and it did not change its nature, it blew as strongly and gusted as fiercely, but now, instead of southerly, it flies from the West. I know this change. I have seen it before. It will fade, slowly, like a poorly written song, from forty, to thirty, to twenty, to ten. The gusts will diminish, sixty, forty-five, thirty, fifteen. Soon, in twenty minutes, maybe an hour, there will be calm. The dust will stop, no longer lifted, and will sift slowly down, to coat the rocks that at this moment lie clean and polished. In the morning I will step out on Mexican soil, successfully immigrated during the night, and here to stay, unless a January Norther deports it. Could happen. It has happened before.

In the calm and the quiet, I return to bed.

Morning. The dull and dim light gleams through fresh and clear air, as clear as the minutes following a spring shower. Nothing moves. A few clouds have flown in from the West, and now trim the eastern horizon, just beginning to pink with the dawn. A tall snag, a long dead palo verde that served as a landmark of my campsite, the hummingbird's favorite lookout, lies prone upon the ground, bridging the wash. Debris lines the brush that lines the wash to the North; it will take me half an hour to clean it up. My neighbor to the West emerges from his car, and surveys what the day before had been his tent. Half of it lies in tatters; the other half is scattered to the horizon. To the South, a dozen men survey a trailer which lies on its side. There will be several such, and the men from the town will bring their machines to set the fallen ones back on their wheels. It is nothing unusual; it may happen two or three times more this winter. There have been injuries, perhaps a few deaths. It is normal, it is expected in this small town whose winter population exceeds a million people, where the average age in the summer is sixty-six, and in the winter, perhaps eighty. It is a small-scale aftermath of a hurricane, in the same sense as a dust-devil is a small-scale tornado. Most of the people slept through it quite comfortably.

But now it is over. It is morning. The storm is spent, and gone with the old year. Forget your arbitrary calendars, this is the Solstice, this is the beginning of Winter, the time of rest and peace. This is the first day of the new year, and it is born with the stupendous glory of a brilliant and magnificent dawn. And the Sun peeks over the horizon.

It will be a glorious year!

About the Author

The Lonesome Hillbilly is a wanderer from birth. Born in the Lone Star Republic (but not in Texas), he traveled a thousand miles by his first birthday, and ten thousand by his second. He lives on a motorcycle, and in a tent he made. He has been in every state of the Union, plus Asia and Europe. Politically he is a Rational Anarchist. Spiritually, he respects all religions, and no churches. He winters in the low deserts of Arizona, and tours all New Mexico during the Spring. The rest of the time, you will find him somewhere within five hundred miles of the Rocky Mountains. Probably.

Stay Free!

www.ingramcontent.com/pod-product-compliance
Lightning Source LLC
Chambersburg PA
CBHW061759250726
48657CB00001B/205